D1560663

Human Capital Management

What Really Works in Government

Human Capital Management

What Really Works in Government

Federal Management Partners, Inc.

MANAGEMENTCONCEPTS PRESS

ʃʃʃ
MANAGEMENTCONCEPTS PRESS
8230 Leesburg Pike, Suite 800
Tysons Corner, VA 22182
(703) 790-9595
Fax: (703) 790-1371
www.managementconcepts.com

Copyright © 2014 by Management Concepts, Inc.

All rights reserved. No part of this book may be reproduced or utilized in any form or by any means, electronic or mechanical, including photocopying, recording, or by an information storage and retrieval system, without permission in writing from the publisher, except for brief quotations in review articles.

Printed in the United States of America

Library of Congress Control Number: 2013947642

ISBN 978-1-56726-428-9

10   9   8   7   6   5   4   3   2   1

Contents

Foreword

The demands being made on a complex, multisectoral workforce delivering public services in the early 21st century call for nimble and innovative government; evidence-based, results-based, and data-driven management; doing more with less; and the expanded use of technology and telecommuting. Trends and trendy solutions abound, but the key to success in meeting these demands is a well-led and well-managed workforce. People represent the most critical resource of all. Mission achievement and a high-performing government are possible only with effective recruitment, development, and retention processes.

While information technology provides support to collect data, it is the people inside government who identify relevant data, interpret and make sense of those data, and inspire others to do well and to do good in government. Innovation in approaches to achieve mission-oriented goals throughout government is valued and needed—and it is the people who innovate and inspire, not the technology.

Given the complexity of the policy environment and today's issues, made only more uncertain by politics, effectively leading and managing government's most critical resource—its employees—presents possibly the most pressing challenge of all. *Human Capital Management: What Really Works in Government* addresses this challenge by offering promising practices in leading and managing people working in government. The authors not only share innovative practices, but they also describe the details of implementation and offer practical advice on addressing likely obstacles. This advice is relevant for public agencies at all levels of government in the United States and most likely abroad as well.

The authors offer solid ideas on recruiting, developing, and retaining good people to conduct the important work of government. Their focus on people as our critical resource is well placed. The authors have carefully analyzed the strategies and tactics they helped design and implement to improve human resource policies and practices in a way that improves organizational learning and performance in a wide variety of settings in the federal government.

The lessons the authors offer ring true for any number of settings. The themes in their stories that call out for attention are the "high-touch" approaches needed for inspiration, interpretation, and innovation in leading and managing people.

People need *inspiration* from enlightened and empowering leadership. Leaders throughout the organization shape the organizational culture; their demonstrated commitment and support for effective human resource practices, and for their employees, are essential. Leaders set the stage for high-performing organizations through clear communications, expectations, incentives, and support for employees—starting with recruitment—and highly in-touch leaders are simply more inspiring.

In an era noted for the tremendous amount of data available within government, employees need training (and both technical and moral support) to ensure that they collect relevant and reliable data, as well as the skills and support to interpret and make sense of those data. *Interpretation* of data and translation of their meaning to make informed and enlightened decisions are essential to improve governmental performance—but this will not simply happen. Committed leadership and enlightened training are clearly necessary to ensure that important data are collected, analyzed, and used to improve performance.

Innovation in the way government does business is essential, and it is within reach. Innumerable innovative approaches to human resource policies and practices, as well as business processes, are being developed in governments across the world. But innovation is most likely to occur through person-to-person interaction, and employees need the space and trust to try new approaches. Fruitful interpretation of data and successful innovation can both be cultivated and nurtured by empowering and inspiring leaders. It always comes back to the people—the people who lead and the leaders they recruit and develop.

The authors of this book offer valuable contributions that can help public managers make progress on the issues facing government today.

—Kathryn Newcomer

Preface

Best practices are like textbooks: They're great for learning. They're great to have in your toolbox of methods and ideas. They provide a wonderfully intellectual framework for beginning to tackle a particular problem or issue. But the negative side of a textbook is what is often referred to as the "textbook solution." A textbook solution honors the theory and ideas presented in the textbook but fails to respond to the particulars of the situation at hand. In that regard, a textbook solution is like an ideology: People adopt the solution because they think they're supposed to, not because it solves the problem they're attempting to solve in the most cost-effective way possible. Another way to think about the textbook solution is that it lacks common sense. It's great in theory, but in practicality, will it work as advertised?

The human capital management profession has sometimes overemphasized best practices. Human capital management can be susceptible to trendiness, to a focus on what's hot and what's not. A quick review of the evolution of some human capital buzzwords is instructive: Personnel management became human resources management and then human capital management; KSAs (knowledge/skills/abilities) became competencies; position management became workforce planning and then succession planning; morale became engagement; pay became compensation; in-processing became onboarding. Even the term *human capital*, which we have chosen to use in this book, is beginning to go out of favor in some circles.

In most cases, we would argue, the evolution these changes in terminology represent was positive—either a way to refresh and energize a good concept or practice that had become stale or a real leap forward in thinking about how to achieve certain goals or solve certain problems. But still there remains the element of trendiness, of emphasizing image and perception over reality, in human capital management.

It may seem unusual to start a book on best practices by downplaying the very notion of best practices, but we believe that doing so helps put our approach in the proper context. Use the information in this book for what it is—ideas to learn from and to stimulate your thinking. But don't use the information formulaically to solve all your human capital problems. Using this approach also helped us set a standard for ourselves in writing this book. In trying to identify and articulate human capital best practices in the federal government, we want to avoid the prescriptive approach, the follow-these-seven-easy-steps approach. We want to be rich on complexity and context. We want to describe what really happened in an agency when its leaders and staff used that best practice. What particular conditions contributed to the agency's success or failure in applying the practice? How did the agency adapt the practice to make it work in a particular situation? Ultimately, we want to go beyond the glossy image to the reality that underlies the best practice. We want to uncover the messy, practical difficulties and challenges that agencies were able to overcome and explore how they did that—how they were able to conquer their particular reality.

To accomplish this goal, we organized our book around a series of case studies that showcase how particular agencies have achieved significant results through the application of human capital best practices. The case studies span all aspects of the human capital lifecycle—from how agencies have recruited and hired the talent they need to accomplish their mission, to how agencies have developed the competencies their workforce needs to be successful and grow professionally, to how agencies have inspired and led their workforce to perform at the highest levels and participate enthusiastically in the life of the organization.

The chapters are written by a variety of staff from Federal Management Partners, Inc. (FMP), who worked closely with each agency to bring the stories to life. Although we weren't prescriptive in our approach, each case study follows this general outline:

- What was the issue the agency needed to solve?

- What process did the agency use to come up with the solution?

- What are the nuts and bolts of how the solution works?

- What specific, measurable improvements resulted from the solution?

- How smoothly did the implementation and change process go and what strategies were used for change?

- What would the agency have done differently and what further improvements are anticipated?

- What two or three ingredients made this solution successful for the agency?

As we were developing these case studies, we began to see some common themes that enabled each agency to succeed. In our concluding chapter, we step back to take a broader view by focusing on these themes. In many cases, the specific technical features of the best practice proved less important than the way the agency went about building and implementing it. If we could bottle any one overall best practice and prescribe it, it would probably be represented in those themes.

Through our experience, we have learned that sometimes human capital professionals can become myopic. They may come to see their organization through a localized lens that narrows their vision. In this book, we present some though-provoking human capital ideas and possibilities—from a powerful story about how the Department of Transportation's Office of the Inspector General fundamentally changed its leadership culture and blazed a trail for dramatic organizational change; to how the Customs and Border Protection Bureau used metrics, coupled with creative thinking and an unwavering focus on a single goal, to dramatically increase the size of its workforce by nearly 50 percent in just 18 months; to how the U.S. Patent and Trademark Office implemented a telework program that resulted in major contributions to the bottom line. If we've done our job well, you will be able to see exactly how these agencies applied particular human capital best practices in their unique organizational environment to achieve these results, and how you can apply them to solve the problems and issues your organization faces. In the end, we hope the real value of this book is that it enables you to try on a new lens and to expand your horizons—to realize, "I hadn't thought of that before. Maybe that would work for me."

—*Erin Pitera*

Acknowledgments

This book represents a group effort, and the group is large. It includes leaders and professionals from over a dozen different federal agencies, most of the consulting staff at FMP, several esteemed human capital professionals external to but closely associated with FMP, and of course the publisher, Management Concepts. We can't begin to do justice to what each has contributed, but we'll try.

- *Department of Transportation, Office of the Inspector General.* Thanks to Calvin Scovel (Inspector General), Ann Calvaresi-Barr (Deputy Inspector General), and Susan Dailey (Assistant Inspector General for Administration) for graciously sharing the details of what they have accomplished to strengthen the OIG's leadership and organizational culture.

- *United States Agency for International Development.* Thanks to Dr. Robert Baker (management analyst and team lead, OHR/PPIM/Planning), George Thompson, P.E. (senior human resources advisor, OHR/PPIM/ Planning), and the rest of the Office of Human Resources planning team for their vision, leadership, and creativity in building and implementing a best-in-class workforce planning tool.

- *Customs and Border Protection.* Thanks to Robert Hosenfeld (former Assistant Commissioner for Human Resources) for sharing data and telling the exciting story of one of the major staffing successes in recent memory.

- *National Science Foundation.* Thanks to Cary Kemp Larson (New Executive Transition program manager),

Marilyn Dickman (former Deputy Director of Human Resource Management), and Emily Herchen (former project manager) for their leadership and support in transforming NSF's onboarding programs.

- *Center for Veterinary Medicine.* Thanks to Jackie Salter, Shannon Bradbury, April Jones-Tate, Heather Weiser, and Brooke Mulkins for their vision, leadership, and continued dedication to CVM's best-in-class onboarding program.

- *Department of Veterans Affairs.* Thanks to VA for the opportunity to share the vision of its remarkable and ongoing human capital initiatives. With programs like MyCareer@VA and VA for Vets, VA has offered tremendous leadership in the areas of employee engagement and development.

- *Patent and Trademark Office.* Thanks to Danette Campbell (telework senior advisor) for enthusiastically sharing USPTO's history and accomplishments with telework.

- *Flight Standards Service.* Thanks to Chris Heizer (assistant Training Division manager) and Deborah Stephenson (manager, Integrated Curriculum branch) for recounting the long journey FSS has made to transform its technical training curriculum.

- *Social Security Administration.* Thanks to Reginald Wells (Deputy Commissioner for Human Resources), Ralph Patinella (Acting Associate Commissioner for Labor-Management and Employee Relations), Wanda M. Jones (Acting Deputy Associate Commissioner for Labor-Management and Employee Relations), Kathy Jeffries (Executive Officer, Office of Human Resources), Jim Parikh (Center Director for Program Policy, Automation, and Training), and Chris Bowser (human resource specialist).

- *National Geospatial-Intelligence Agency.* Thanks to the agency for supporting us in telling the story of its award-winning HR system built on pay bands and performance pay.

- *Air Force Research Laboratory.* Thanks to Michelle Williams (Director, Demonstration Project Office), who has lived contribution-based compensation for over a decade, for sharing her observations and insights into the contribution-based compensation concept and its impact at AFRL.

- *National Archives and Records Administration.* Thanks to Analisa Archer (former Chief Human Capital Officer), Deborah Dodson (Acting Chief Human Capital Officer, and Director, Human Capital Planning and Accountability), Lisa Ratnavale (former Business Systems manager), and Constance Jodon (Director of Talent Management) for contributing their perspectives on transforming a traditional human resources function to a more modern, strategic partner within the agency.

- *National Aeronautics and Space Administration.* Thanks to Jeri Buchholz (Chief Human Capital Officer) for championing the NASA success story and to Candace Irwin (former Director, Workforce Systems and Accountability Division), Michael Stewart (lead for the Human Resources Information Systems team), and Daniel Costello (Workforce Systems team) for providing us with the history and context of their systems and for continuing to promote HR technology excellence at NASA.

- *Department of Labor.* Thanks to Alvin "Chip" Black (Director, Office of HR Systems) and Albert Sloane (Director, benefits.gov) for providing their valuable insights related to change management and communications efforts for supporting large-scale HR technology implementations.

- *National Institutes of Health.* Thanks to Phil Lenowitz (Deputy Director, Office of Human Resources) for providing detailed data and valuable insights into the critical elements of success in delivering both strategic and operational excellence.

We have worked closely with many of these federal leaders and their staffs on the initiatives described in this book. Some started out as FMP's clients; others were introduced to us through the process of writing this book. We consider all of them our partners and associates in the continuing effort to create and implement effective, efficient, world-class best practices across the federal government. They have contributed overwhelmingly to the stories and case studies related in this book, freely sharing their thoughts and insights; their comments are their own and do not purport to represent their agencies. We can't thank them enough. Of course, any errors or omissions are the authors' own; we hope our contributors and readers will let us know if there's anything we've haven't gotten quite right.

In addition to the FMP authors identified in each chapter and highlighted at the end of the book in *About the Authors*, we would like to acknowledge Justin Weis for editing and assembling the case studies presented in this book. In addition, most of the consulting staff at FMP were involved in some way in one or more of the book's chapters by tracking down information, providing insight and ideas, reviewing drafts, assembling data, and any number of other important tasks that go into the development of a book like this. As always, FMP's staff is the secret to everything we do.

We consider FMP to be a community, and that entire community was instrumental in writing this book. Some in the FMP community helped us directly by authoring all or part of a chapter. Specific acknowledgements go out to Dr. Kathryn Newcomer of George Washington University for writing the foreword, Paul Thompson for playing a lead role in writing Chapter 8, Ilona Birenbaum for contributing her insights and experiences related to Chapter 1, and Robert Hosenfeld, former assistant commissioner for human resources at Customs and Border Protection.

In addition to these direct contributors, others in the FMP community played major roles in helping us conceptualize the book, identify cases studies, and track down people and information. Special thanks go to Kathryn Medina, OPM Executive Director of the CHCO council; Dan Blair, President and CEO of the National Academy of Public Administration; and Myra Howze Shiplett, President of Randolph Morgan Consulting and a Fellow of the National Academy of Public Administration.

Finally, Management Concepts has been endlessly tolerant of our new and changing ideas for the book, our delays, and our ignorance of all that goes into an endeavor such as this. Thanks to Myra Strauss for holding our hand through the process.

Developing New Leaders

Department of Transportation, Office of the Inspector General

Tim Barnhart
Lisa Sper
Jessica Dzieweczynski

The more than 70 Offices of Inspector General (OIG) in the federal government all have a similar mission: to conduct independent audits and investigations for their respective department's programs and operations to promote economy, effectiveness, and efficiency and to prevent and detect fraud, waste, and abuse. OIGs keep Congress, department heads, and the American taxpayer fully informed about deficiencies related to the administration of programs and operations and offer corrective actions that help protect and strengthen departmental results. In short, they are agency watchdogs and stewards of taxpayer dollars.

Late in 2006, Calvin L. Scovel III became the sixth Inspector General (IG) at the Department of Transportation (DOT). By all measures, the DOT OIG was a successful organization when Cal arrived. It had earned the respect of Congress, the department, and the IG community. But Cal soon recognized that to sustain this level of performance, the office needed to do more. Cal's 29 years of service in the U.S. Marine Corps, where he retired as Brigadier General, helped influence his vision.

Cal describes his vision for leadership at OIG this way: "A common Marine Corps slogan is 'Mission First; People Always.' To achieve our mission, we needed to continually develop a high-performing group of people. It was the people part of the slogan I felt we needed to focus on at OIG. I am a firm believer that if senior leaders pay more attention to staff, mission performance will be elevated. I often refer to the three T's: training, tools, and time. Staff need training to perform and grow, tools to perform efficiently, and time to apply the training and tools effectively. I knew we had a lot of work ahead, but we also needed to show patience to allow our actions to have effect."

DOT Office of Inspector General

The Department of Transportation's OIG is committed to fulfilling its statutory responsibilities and supporting members of Congress, the secretary, senior department officials, and the public in achieving a safe, efficient, and effective transportation system. In fiscal year 2012, OIG issued 188 audit reports with 589 recommendations, including financial recommendations totaling $1.8 billion, and testified eight times before Congress. OIG's investigative work resulted in 145 indictments, 95 convictions, and more than $32 million in fines, restitutions, and recoveries. Ultimately, for every dollar appropriated to DOT OIG in fiscal year 2012, the office returned more than $23.

A critical indicator of OIG's organizational culture was the federal human capital survey (now the federal employee viewpoint survey), which measures employees' perceptions of conditions characterizing successful organizations and which the Partnership for Public Service uses to calculate its index of best places to work. Dissatisfied with OIG's 2006 survey scores, Cal made it a visible priority for his leadership team to address the issues highlighted by the survey, specifically leadership, performance culture, and employee satisfaction. By 2011, OIG had improved its scores dramatically, with trends continuing in 2012. The office landed in the top 25 percent on the best places to work index, making it the second most improved subcomponent organization in the federal government. Figure 1-1 highlights the transformation.

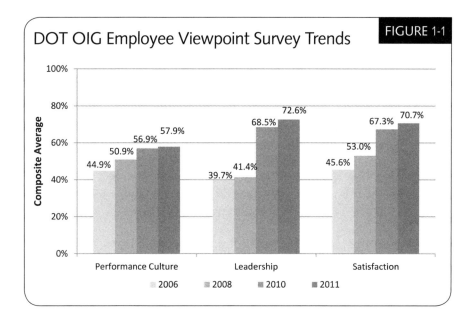

The story of how OIG accomplished these results abounds with useful best practices and strategies for change.

Focus on Developing Leaders

While Cal didn't have a step-by-step plan to achieve his vision for change, he knew where he wanted to end up and he was comfortable with figuring out the route along the way. To help plot this route, Cal enlisted Ilona Birenbaum as a consultant in 2007. "One of the reasons this worked," according to Ilona, "was that Cal was so flexible. Nothing was locked in but the end vision. He would try something, learn from that, improve it, and try again. Cal had a humble approach, and I think that demonstrated a lot of integrity to the staff. He showed a clear determination to change things, and he invited everyone to help him get there."

Cal started with his immediate team of senior executives. Ilona describes their approach and success factors:

We conducted a 360 degree assessment of each of the senior executives, including Cal. It was a pretty traditional 360 approach. We created a leadership competency model that reflected Cal's vision and we used those competencies as the basis of the assessment. We did a few things that made the process work especially well. First, we spent a lot of time before the assessment communicating the purpose of the assessment and orienting the raters to their role and what we were asking from them—why we needed honest feedback, how it would be used, and how anonymity would be preserved. We also spent time with the executives, coaching them on how to receive and assess the feedback. I think that investment paid off handsomely.

Another thing we did that worked well was a facilitated debrief of the assessment results with the executives and their supervisors. This was part of the accountability piece. We wanted both the executive and the executive's supervisor to understand the issues and agree to them. We wanted both individuals to commit to a development plan and milestones for addressing the feedback. In other words, we wanted the executives to take the feedback seriously. In addition, we tied completion of the development plan to the executive's performance plan. Their performance ratings would be based in part on their diligence in addressing the weaknesses identified through the 360. These decisions definitely got the executives' attention.

Coaching was the central element of each executive's development plan. "We really emphasized coaching," Ilona says. "Our coaching model focused almost entirely on the results of the 360. If one executive needed to work on communication, that was the coach's focus. If another needed to delegate and empower, we worked on that. Our method as coaches was to develop a relationship with the executive, set clear and measurable coaching goals, and through regular meetings, work to leverage their leadership strengths and address their gaps. We assigned executives homework, which included reflection, practice, and reading to create opportunities to strengthen the skills they actively were working on. For example, executives who struggled with difficult conversations were asked to hold these conversations and reflect on what went well and what didn't go well. Then the next coaching session would focus on that experience."

OIG began to see immediate impacts of the assessment and coaching. Internal survey scores began to go up and coaching participants relayed extremely positive feedback on the coaching experience.

Leadership Transformation – Keys to Success

1) Executive Commitment
   - Vision
   - Flexibility
   - Inclusiveness
   - Patience

2) Competency-based Leadership Assessment
   - Clear purpose
   - Understanding of process
   - Assistance with receiving feedback

3) Accountability
   - Debrief with executive and supervisor
   - Development plan tied to performance
   - Individual coaching
   - Focus on behavior change

The emphasis on strengthening leadership continued with the arrival of Ann Calvaresi Barr in 2009. Ann, who is currently the Deputy Inspector General, spearheaded many new initiatives aimed at enhancing OIG's work processes and motivating its workforce. Ann describes the beginnings of culture change at OIG:

> Once everyone saw we were committed to changing the organizational culture, people came to *expect* good leadership and to demand it. We actively sought employee input, and we kept getting great suggestions and ideas for what we could accomplish. Coaching was key to our efforts, but it was just the beginning.

The dramatic change we saw is attributable more to an infectious spirit that impacted our people and our work. That was the real change. And that change came straight from Cal. He modeled and expected good leadership, and everyone followed naturally.

We've also been highly data-based in our approach. The key metric we watched was OPM's employee viewpoint survey scores. We wanted those scores to keep going up, and they have. In addition to OPM's survey, we developed a supplemental survey that we administer regularly. Our survey allowed us to delve deeper into leadership and organizational performance to make sure we were progressing according to Cal's vision. We also conducted numerous employee focus groups to get behind the data and identify what specifically triggered certain survey responses, especially those that changed significantly or still needed attention. The focus group input helped us identify what was needed to maintain and further build a motivated workforce and a high-performing organization.

After the initial 360 assessment and coaching, OIG initiated a number of specific efforts:

- *Training.* The 360 assessments identified consistent learning needs across OIG's leadership and management team. To augment the coaching, OIG developed a three-part supervisor training series. *Supervision I* focuses on human resource management, performance management, and providing feedback. *Supervision II* focuses on conflict management, team development, and collaboration. *Supervision III* focuses on emotional intelligence, vision, leading change, and managing stress. OIG began offering this training in 2010 to all managers and supervisors in the organization. In addition, OIG offered targeted training focused on self-awareness, self-management, social awareness, and relationship management. Myers-Briggs Type Indicator® (MBTI®) workshops were also offered to help teams understand individual differences and improve communication, teamwork, and collaboration.

Ann describes the momentum generated by these activities:

> Once we got rolling, the ideas for various types of training and workshops just exploded. With Cal's full support, we started a speaker series and organized communities of practice, where staff share knowledge and lessons learned to broaden perspectives and encourage greater coordination and partnering on OIG's work. We also started monthly leadership brownbags that bring OIG managers and executives together to focus on topics of mutual interest. Topics have included managing diversity and inclusivity, traits of an effective leader, performance management, and motivating and engaging staff. What I love about the brownbags is that they allow me to connect with all the managers in the organization, to hear how they see things and what they struggle with. We've had strong participation in the leadership brownbags. In fact, they became so popular that staff asked us to do something similar for employees at all levels of the organization, which we called leadership development exchanges. Since October 2011, we have held leadership development exchanges on topics such as adaptability and communication strategies, cultivating trust, managing conflict, and leading across organizational units.

> Other opportunities for training came in the form of organizational self-assessment. Calling on best practices from his military days, Cal instituted the "hot wash," a type of learning debrief where Cal meets with teams immediately after a congressional hearing and other major work accomplishments to discuss what worked, what didn't, what they learned, and what they would change. We also instituted return on investment meetings, led by Lou Dixon, Principal Assistant Inspector General

for Auditing and Evaluation, to look critically at the returns we were able to achieve through a particular audit or evaluation.

The enthusiasm for learning is pretty strong around here. When staff see that self-assessment and learning are important to the leadership, they find dozens of ways to accomplish them.

- *Mentoring.* OIG began a comprehensive employee mentoring program to create a one-of-a-kind opportunity for individual or group collaboration, goal achievement, and problem-solving. Consistent with OIG's motto, "Mission First, People Always," the mentoring program provides staff with a developmental partnership where knowledge, skills, information, and perspectives are shared to foster personal and professional growth. All employees are eligible to participate, and many do. Mentors serve as role models or coaches as they share career information and insight from their own work and life experience. Mentees take a brief survey to help match them with an appropriate mentor. Both mentors and mentees receive training to help them structure the process and clarify expectations.

- *Leadership planning and collaboration.* One of Cal's first steps as IG was to engage his senior staff in a discussion on how to achieve his vision. OPM's viewpoint survey and other data informed this discussion. A human capital council was formed to identify critical people needs and issues OIG faced and what was needed to further strengthen its capabilities. Senior staff were empowered to monitor their progress toward Cal's leadership vision and to identify the need for changes in the plans and tactics for getting there. The leadership team also came together to develop a comprehensive strategic plan for OIG; that plan has since been updated, with a focus on clearly defining the results it is seeking to accomplish and developing clear measures of its success in achieving those results. Leaders work together to develop and continually reevaluate tactical plans for how OIG's audits and investigations will achieve its broader strategic objectives to identify deficiencies in DOT programs and operations and to examine allegations of fraud, waste, and abuse.

- *Performance culture*. Performance management quickly emerged as a critical area where change was warranted. Traditionally, line managers had developed performance plans for each employee. There was little consistency or integration across the plans or alignment with the strategic goals of the organization. As the leadership team began to clarify and define strategic goals through its strategic planning activities, OIG built on that strategic framework to define performance expectations for critical occupations and roles. Performance plans were developed with clear, measurable objectives for auditors, investigators, analysts, and mission support staff.

  Recently, OIG updated position descriptions and standards, and enhanced metrics to hold staff accountable. OIG also rolled out training for managers on how to have critical conversations with staff on performance expectations, how to address poor performance, how to provide effective feedback, and how to help their workforce with career planning.

  In addition, OIG implemented "skip-level" feedback sessions, which are discussions between a supervisor's boss and the supervisor's direct report—without the supervisor present. These sessions proved extremely useful in assessing the performance of supervisors and helped OIG's leadership understand broad performance challenges across the organization. Most important, they were consistent with Cal's determination to have senior staff understand the impact of their leadership behavior and actions, as well as his focus on accountability.[1]

- *Communication*. A key element of Cal's vision was open and honest communication. He wanted the entire workforce to be connected and to understand where they were going as an organization, how they were performing, and where they needed to improve. Cal notes, "One thing I learned early in my career is that if you want good information flowing to you as a leader, then you never shoot the messenger. My door is always open. I really need to hear and learn from my staff."

One of the first actions Cal took was to hold all-hands meetings every six months, with webcasting to all OIG offices. The goal of these meetings, and Cal's approach in general, is to be as transparent as possible to staff about the challenges OIG faces, what is being done to respond to those challenges, and what employees can expect, with ample time allotted for questions. For example, during a time of governmentwide budget constraints, Cal was forthright in communicating possible budget scenarios and how employees might be affected. He sent regular emails to staff whenever new situations developed or important information needed to be communicated. OIG also started a weekly newsletter, *The Inspector*, which provides timely reports on congressional hearings, audit and investigative work, external recognition and awards, speakers, and a forum for staff to get to know one another better.

Cal holds regular meetings with his key executives. He includes his leaders in decision-making whenever possible and, if he needs to make decisions independently, he fully communicates why those decisions were necessary and works with his leaders to implement them effectively. Finally, Cal and other executives routinely meet with staff on their work. These activities have become a part of how the OIG leadership does business.

A Harder Look

In addition to these development and communication initiatives, OIG conducted a number of organizational assessments that looked at the performance, organization, and culture of specific organizational components within OIG. These assessments provided a deeper, richer understanding of the issues and led to initiatives to improve processes and clarify roles. For example, the processes OIG uses to develop and review audit reports were streamlined to encourage collaboration throughout the design and writing stages. Senior reviewers were encouraged to provide constructive feedback that focused on higher level messaging and problem-solving. OIG developed templates, guidelines, and other standardized tools to assist staff with the new processes. Through these initiatives, the quality and timeliness of the audit reports have improved. Similarly, new priorities and protocols established under the leadership of Tim Barry, Principal Assistant Inspector General for Investigations, have helped ensure that OIG's investigative case work has the greatest impact on the department's primary mission to ensure safety as well as deter and eliminate fraud, waste, and abuse.

But the most important lesson that came out of the organizational assessments was that OIG needed to continue to shine a bright light on leadership. Ilona notes that Cal didn't simply provide training for his leaders and declare the job done:

> He made it clear that leadership performance and behavior *had* to change. After the initial wave of 360 feedback and coaching, some leaders were able to change and some weren't. When we went back in and did the organizational assessments, we saw where change had occurred and where it was still business as usual. It was at that point that Cal reiterated his expectations to selected leaders. As a result, there was some turnover, allowing OIG to bring in new leaders who would have the skills and model the values Cal wanted.

Cal shares his perspective:

> One of the most important things I did was to *not* bring in *my* people, the people I knew and had worked with over the course of my career. They were outstanding leaders, and I knew they would bring great strengths, but I wanted us to change, largely with the people we had. I wanted us to own the change and the new leadership. Many of our new leaders have come from with-

in. We picked the best internal people, then we brought in some outstanding leaders from outside our office following a rigorous interview and assessment process. But in the end, they were *our* leaders, not *my* leaders. That was important.

Ilona adds her thoughts:

We did some excellent things to help develop leaders, and I know they had an impact. But anyone setting out to fundamentally change the leadership culture of an organization needs to be prepared to go back to the drawing board. I don't think a learning and development strategy alone is enough in most cases. Sooner or later, you have to make sure you've got the right people with the right skill sets to lead the organization.

Internal Leadership and Support

OIG also realized that change is continual and it is hard work. Change requires time and resources, and it can't be allowed to slip down on the priority list. As the scope and magnitude of the changes became apparent to OIG, it also became clear that the office needed a strong support staff to help plan the change strategy, manage the many initiatives that were being launched, support communications, and monitor the data and the effectiveness of the initiatives.

Cal relied on Susan Dailey, Assistant Inspector General for Administration, to lead the business operations group, which includes human resources, budget and finance, contracting, and information technology. Susan had worked as an auditor in OIG, so she understood the organization well and what business support was needed to be effective. She also believed in Cal's vision and was enthusiastic about moving it forward.

Susan describes the changed mindset in her group:

> One of the first things I realized was that we needed people with a different set of skills who could understand a general goal and translate it into a specific plan. We needed people who worked together to provide the services that leaders and managers required. The "training, tools, and time" concept that Cal talked about resonated with everyone. Our job was to provide the training and the tools as well as to help manage the overall change process. I think the most important thing we did was enhance our training curriculum. The coaching got us started, then the training followed and helped us reach all the way across our management team. Before we started the supervisory training program, our managers had little training in leadership and management. They were good auditors and investigators but needed to understand more about the intricacies and nuances, the "art" of leading people. If I were doing it over, I would move up the supervisory training to the beginning of the change process.

Susan's team took the lead in implementing specific organizational initiatives, including training, surveys, and coaching. "In the beginning, I felt I was driving things forward with my team," says Susan. "I would come up with the ideas, lay out goals and plans, and try to get all my people to understand what they needed to do to successfully implement those plans. But now it's completely different. Now they tell me what needs to be done. They've taken this process over and are driving it themselves. That, more than anything else, is a testament to the quality and talent of the people we've brought into operations. It's a phenomenal team."

Another key lesson was that the responsibility for change can't be delegated. Cal says, "Once things were going in the right direction, I thought I could step back from the changes we were trying to make, but I quickly learned that my involvement and attention were still essential. People needed to know that I still cared about this. That was an important lesson for me. I couldn't just check it off my to-do list and move on to other things. It had to become a part of my daily life, in much the same way I was asking everyone else to make it part of their daily lives."

What Has Changed

The federal employee viewpoint survey scores were a key catalyst that helped OIG realize it had to change, and they are one of the best indicators of the positive effects the change efforts have had on the organization. But there are other strong indicators of progress as well:

- *Return on investment.* OIG calculates the return on investment (ROI) for every taxpayer dollar it spends on audits and investigations. Cal says, "In 2008, the Government Accountability Office (GAO) reported on all OIGs' monetary accomplishments as stated in its semiannual reports to Congress for fiscal year 2007. DOT OIG's overall return was $15 for every $1 spent— the third best in the government. But I believed our efforts to improve our organization and culture would benefit our ROI. While GAO hasn't done another study, we track our own ROI. In 2012, our ROI was $23 to $1. We've stepped up our focus on 'Mission First,' but the 'People Always' part is what allowed us to do that. The team here is extremely high-performing."

- *Workforce retention.* Historically, the rate of attrition in OIG was running between 8 and 14 percent. In 2012, attrition slowed to 4 percent. A slow economy may have had something to do with that change, but surveys indicated that OIG has also created an organization that people like being a part of. OIG has created a climate that attracts and retains the very best talent in government.

- *Organizational climate.* Life at OIG has changed in ways that are not easily measured but are nevertheless palpable. OIG leaders and managers comment on the impact of these changes:

○ "We've absorbed some significant budget cuts each of the past two years but remain highly productive. I can't imagine the impact those budget cuts would've had if we hadn't turned around our organizational culture."

○ "Employees give us good feedback. They love the training. They love the communication mechanisms we've set up. People are saying good things."

○ "There's accountability now—positive accountability. People aren't blaming each other when things go wrong; they're looking at themselves to figure out what they can do to deliver the results we need. It's self-accountability."

○ "We're working together more effectively. We broke down many of the silos, and staff now look for opportunities to work on cross-organizational initiatives. There's less competition and more collaboration."

Why It Worked

OIG leaders did just about everything they could do to change things and to keep the momentum of change moving forward. As Ilona Birenbaum noted, the 360 assessment and coaching were incredibly powerful, but if the office had done only that, the results would likely have been minor. They didn't stop there. They rolled out a complete leadership development program. They worked on OIG's performance culture. They worked on communication. They rethought their business processes. They built an operational infrastructure to support the changes they pursued. One of the most important ingredients in their success was their willingness to attack on all fronts. They didn't see the challenge as one problem with one solution, but as many problems with many solutions. As a result, OIG was able to implement and reap the rewards of profound, significant change.

Ilona says, "I think the most important thing they did was make tough decisions about leaders. They didn't merely talk about problems, they took action. They secured the right leaders and they held everyone accountable."

Susan shares her thoughts for what led to OIG's success: "Cal gave it time. That was the most important thing to me. He didn't have a 90-day plan or a 180-day plan; there wasn't a timeline. He had a firm vision and a rock-solid commitment to achieve that vision, no matter how long it took. That's why it worked."

Ann adds, "I think this worked because we listened well. We were able to get a good read on the organization and track how we were progressing. We continually played back what we were seeing and hearing and got validation from the workforce on what was going on. People were engaged. Continual listening, validating, and responding with process and operations improvements that address root causes of concerns is time-consuming but absolutely essential for our success, or any organization's success."

And finally, Cal himself says, "We have an incredible group of leaders in place. Each and every one of them has been critical to our success. To ensure we are meeting our mission while operating at peak efficiency, I rely on my senior executives: Ann, my deputy; Susan, who stays on top of our operations; Lou Dixon, who heads up our audits; Tim Barry, who leads our investigative work; and Brian Dettelbach, our Assistant Inspector General for Legal, Legislative, and External Affairs. This team and our senior leaders have put in place key initiatives to strengthen our work with a focus on continual improvement."

The Office of Inspector General at the Department of Transportation has made incredible changes over the past five years. New leadership made it happen—new leadership with determination, patience, a focus on its people, a willingness to listen, a readiness to invest, and a penchant for measuring and self-assessment. It's a powerful story that any leader—any organization in government or elsewhere—can learn from. It blazes a trail for dramatic organizational transformation we should all strive to follow.

NOTE

1 While skip-level feedback worked well for OIG and has been documented to work well for many other organizations, it can backfire if not managed skillfully. Other organizations that may be interested in this approach should proceed cautiously by ensuring that the purpose of the skip levels is clearly understood within the organizations and that facilitators of the process remain neutral and do not advocate for any specific outcomes.

A Model for Workforce Planning

U.S. Agency for International Development

Carolyn Kurowski
John Salamone
Ashley Agerter Raitor

The United States Agency for International Development (USAID) has developed and refined a comprehensive strategic workforce planning model that it applies annually to understand its staffing requirements across the entire agency—in its regional and country offices overseas as well as its domestic headquarters. The model is web-based and is accessible to all USAID managers. It draws on critical strategic data within the agency, including budget plans and priorities, country characteristics, and programmatic requirements, to develop targeted staffing levels for the agency and its components, including workforce segments. The model also includes "what-if" features that allow managers to determine the impact of different strategic assumptions on staffing. USAID has been using the model for over ten years and has steadily refined it so that it is now an ingrained management tool. Both the U.S. Office of Management and Budget (OMB) and the U.S. Office of Personnel Management (OPM) have lauded the model and the useful way it informs staffing discussions.

Perhaps the biggest and highest impact change USAID has achieved is a shift to data-based discussions of staffing. Far too often, staffing discussions become internal political battles— contests over whose function or organization is perceived as more important or more in favor—with limited critical assessment of the bottom-line staffing requirements necessary to achieve important strategic results. At USAID, the tenor of staffing discussions has shifted 180 degrees. The real questions are about the agency's strategic requirements. Aided by the model, staffing flows directly out of that strategic understanding in a highly objective, neutral way, facilitating agreement and acceptance among internal managers.

The design and ongoing refinement of USAID's model offer clear best practices that other agencies could leverage. Although extensive analysis would be required to adapt the tool to the specific strategic environment of another agency, the architecture of the model is easily transportable. As with many best practices, the important lessons to be learned are less in the final product than in the journey the organization took to get there.

About USAID

Following the success of the Marshall Plan and the Truman administration's Point Four Program, President John F. Kennedy signed the Foreign Assistance Act in 1961, creating the United States Agency for International Development. Since its inception, USAID has been the leading U.S. agency for providing assistance to countries recovering from natural disasters, trying to escape poverty, and engaging in democratic reforms. By diminishing these underlying conditions, which are often linked to instability and terrorism, USAID plays a vital role in achieving and maintaining national security.

The agency comprises a large, diverse, and distributed workforce. USAID administers foreign aid through a decentralized and relatively complex staffing structure. Employing over 10,000 staff, the agency is headquartered in Washington, DC, and operates in approximately 100 countries across sub-Saharan Africa, Asia, the Middle East, Latin America, and the Caribbean, as well as Europe and Eurasia. From health officers fighting malaria in sub-Saharan Africa to democracy officers promoting free and fair elections in Egypt and Tunisia, USAID's success depends on its ability to assess, manage, and leverage its unique, dedicated, and highly skilled workforce effectively and strategically.

Setting the Context

In August 2003, the U.S. Government Accountability Office (GAO) released a report to Congress that identified human capital management as a high-risk area at USAID, given the agency's primarily ad hoc approach to workforce planning. At the time of GAO's study, USAID was in a period of transition, having evolved from "an agency of U.S. direct-hires that largely provided direct, hands-on implementation of development projects to one that manages and oversees the activities of contractors and grantees....this trend has affected USAID's ability to implement its foreign assistance program as the number of U.S. direct-hire foreign service officers declined and much of USAID's direct-hire workforce was replaced by foreign national personal services contractors." (GAO-03-946, 6) In fact, the number of USAID direct-hires decreased by over 60 percent from 1962 (8,600 direct-hires) to 1990 (3,162 direct-hires). This period was followed by a reduction in force and hiring freeze in the mid-1990s, which further depleted the agency's cadre of direct-hire staff, creating a heavy reliance on contractor support.

GAO further reported that several human capital vulnerabilities resulted from USAID's not having a strategic workforce planning system in place during this period to help manage the transition and anticipate future requirements. For example, "increased attrition of U.S. direct-hires since the reduction in force in the mid-1990s led to the loss of the most experienced foreign service officers, while the hiring freeze stopped the pipeline of new hires at the junior level. The shortage of junior and mid-level officers to staff frontline jobs and a number of unfilled positions have created difficulties...." (GAO-03-946, 14) In addition, GAO reported that USAID lacked the necessary surge capacity, which is imperative for an agency that responds to unpredictable events and changing political environments.

To address these vulnerabilities, GAO challenged USAID to develop and implement a strategic workforce planning process that would mitigate human capital risks and plan for the future of the agency. The question is: How does an organization implement an effective workforce planning process for an interdisciplinary, globally dispersed workforce, ensuring that it is equipped to respond to political upheaval, natural disasters, and economic meltdowns in an ever-changing international landscape?

USAID's Consolidated Workforce Planning Model

In response to GAO's report, USAID's Policy, Planning, and Information Management (PPIM) division initiated a comprehensive workforce planning effort, with the goal of putting the *right people* in the *right place* at the *right time*. PPIM quickly realized that to achieve that goal, a consistent model was needed to help it make institution-wide decisions regarding staffing. USAID developed the consolidated workforce planning model (CWPM), a web-based strategic management tool that uses assumptions based on strategic direction, subject matter expert ratings of diplomatic importance and development potential, funding data, and a variety of additional data-driven assumptions to predict the agency's staffing requirements. While the tool has changed dramatically during its nearly 10-year existence, it remains guided by three critical design precepts:

1. *Build for the future.* The CWPM is a future-oriented tool that projects staffing needs and offers flexibility in response to changing circumstances. The model can be adjusted to reflect a variety of organizational, business, and staffing scenarios. For instance, the number and type of program funding can be adjusted up or down and the model will project the corresponding staffing requirements across different functions. This flexibility has enabled USAID's leaders to consider the workforce implications of changes in both the internal and external environments.

2. *Consider the entire workforce.* As its name conveys, the *consolidated* workforce planning model encompasses USAID's entire, globally dispersed workforce. The tool includes a robust set of assumptions that project foreign service officers (FSOs), general schedule (GS) employees, foreign service nationals (FSNs), those on personal service contracts (PSCs) with the U.S. government, and other types of employees. The model takes into account USAID's use of a variety of employment mechanisms to meet its various staffing needs; a core assumption is that the different employment categories present a unique set of staffing requirements. For instance, direct-hire employees should ideally be performing the long-term work of the organization while PSCs and other special employment mechanisms should be used to meet highly technical or specialized needs over a limited period of time.

3. *Begin with the baseline.* At its core, the model is a complex set of premises and assumptions about USAID's

Example CWPM Workload Drivers and Assumptions

- *Base staffing*: The CWPM assumes that certain functions and roles (e.g., senior managers, administrative staff) are common across all organizational units, regardless of the technical work performed by the unit. These functions are projected using standardized staffing ratios (e.g., one senior manager for every X staff managed).

- *Technical staffing*: The CWPM contains dozens of unique assumptions and formulae that project workload for functions and roles that are unique to a particular organizational unit. For example, the workload for procurement staff in USAID's Office of Acquisition and Assistance is driven by the number, type, and size of contracts managed, while key drivers for USAID's regional bureaus (which design, implement, and evaluate regional and country strategies and programs) are the number and size of overseas missions they support.

- *Staff type distribution:* In addition to projecting quantity, the CWPM contains a number of assumptions regarding staffing mix. For example, the CWPM projects a larger proportion of U.S. direct-hire staff in USAID's Africa region compared to the Europe and Eurasia regions, where in-country staffing support is more readily available.

workload. The starting point was existing data and information such as appropriated funds, ratios of staff to program dollars, and external measures of country concerns. Those assumptions are continually being refined to reflect USAID's evolving future state. This involves gathering information from subject matter experts (SMEs), translating the agency's strategic goals into workforce expectations, and vetting the data with agency leadership.

Workforce Analysis

Since the purpose of the tool is to forecast staffing requirements, USAID first needed to understand and identify the primary factors that impact workload. PPIM initiated a comprehensive workforce analysis to predict workload and staffing demands for the future, identify current workforce gaps, and develop solutions to address those gaps. To execute this study, the team conducted interviews and focus groups with various staff, developed and analyzed workload surveys, and benchmarked staffing levels for comparable work functions across the federal government to determine ideal staffing ratios and identify workload trends (Table 2-1).

Beta Model

The project team compiled the results of the workforce analysis and input them into the initial version of the model. The beta run revealed a number of apparent workforce gaps, particularly in the FSO employment category. For example, overages were identified in the PSC category based on the assumption that long-term work should be performed by direct-hire staff versus contractors. The gaps in these areas were indicative of broader workforce issues, including the need to ensure that USAID has sufficient direct-hire staff to serve as effective stewards of the public trust, the need for better training and career opportunities, and the need to transition individuals who are performing long-term responsibilities out of PSC employment categories into more permanent positions.

Table 2-1. Common Workload Analysis Questions and Implications

Common Workload Analysis Questions	Implications
How much variability in time spent on key functions is there among the departments?	If all departments are spending a significant amount of time on the same types of tasks, there may be opportunities to reconfigure staff in order to streamline processes.
Are functions that employees view as most important consistent with management views?	Discrepancies between what employees and managers view as important may indicate a lack of communication or understanding regarding the alignment between job duties and overall mission.
What types of employees are spending time on specific functions?	Discrepancies between career level and functions can suggest a need to realign functions. For example, if higher-level employees are spending too much time on administrative functions, this work may need to be reassigned.
Do employees feel that their workload has increased, decreased, or remained constant?	If respondents indicate that they have experienced an increase in their workload, it may suggest that employees feel stretched and pressured. If employees continue to perceive their workload as increasing for the long term, they may become disengaged and experience burnout. This can affect the organization's ability to retain high-performing staff.

Following the model's inaugural run, it became clear that the agency had developed an innovative tool that could be used to better understand USAID's complex workforce and evolving staffing needs. However, the beta model was limited in terms of its functionality and the precision of information it produced. In addition, the involvement of senior leadership in framing the tool's underlying assumptions—and institutionalizing the tool into broader workforce planning processes—needed increased emphasis.

Enhancements and Modifications

Given the data imperfections and lack of strong buy-in from senior leaders, PPIM kept a relatively close hold on the CWPM and its projections for the first several iterations. Recognizing that both of these aspects were key ingredients in establishing the tool's credibility across the agency, PPIM instituted several important changes to refine the tool's underlying assumptions and increase the engagement of senior leaders and other key players.

In 2008, a paradigm shift in several of the model's core assumptions occurred. In an effort to coordinate USAID's strategy with the national security strategy, PPIM partnered with the Department of Defense to develop new strategic drivers to ensure that the agency had the right number of personnel in countries that were important to the United States' developmental, diplomatic, and security interests, regardless of program funding. As a result, the CWPM began to consider a number of country factors in determining staffing requirements, including economic growth and political stability. The algorithms that underlie these strategic factors leverage data from reputable external sources, including the World Bank Institute, the World Health Organization, and the International Finance Corporation. This new approach was aimed at establishing the tool's credibility with agency leadership and other stakeholders.

In addition to addressing data quality and strategic alignment, PPIM began to recognize that the CWPM's Microsoft Excel-based operating environment posed significant hurdles. At that time, the model existed as a set of interrelated Excel worksheets, which were tied together through complex formulae and references. As the CWPM increased in scope and complexity, it became increasingly difficult to identify and trace formulaic errors. In addition, the file-based design of the original tool limited the model's accessibility to other USAID staff and key stakeholders. This lack of transparency contributed to misperceptions about the tool's underlying data and its intended uses. PPIM routinely received feedback that other USAID staff perceived the CWPM as a "black box." These usability and transparency issues posed significant risks for implementing the tool into broader workforce planning and resource allocation processes across the agency.

Ultimately, USAID required a new tool to mitigate these risks. In 2009, PPIM expanded the team to include more advanced IT skills with the goal of designing and developing a web-enabled solution. The stability, accuracy, and accessibility provided by the online application were key ingredients in the model's successful implementation, allowing PPIM to focus its efforts on leadership buy-in, communication, and training, with the ultimate goal of increasing awareness and acceptance of the tool across the agency.

With its automated maps and charts, sound effects, and other "bells and whistles," the new web-enabled tool was more visually impressive than its Excel-based predecessor (Figure 2-1). However, to ensure that the numbers projected by this flashy new tool were accepted by a wider, non-HR audience, PPIM needed to identify and establish champions who would advocate for the tool, align its assumptions with the agency's strategic vision, and position its results in a meaningful way.

In 2010, PPIM established the CWPM steering committee. This committee comprises key leadership from HR and other areas of the agency, including the Office of the Administrator. The committee meets regularly to "ground-truth" the model's results, review and authorize major updates to the assumptions and workload drivers, and ensure that the tool reflects current policies, statutes, and strategic direction.

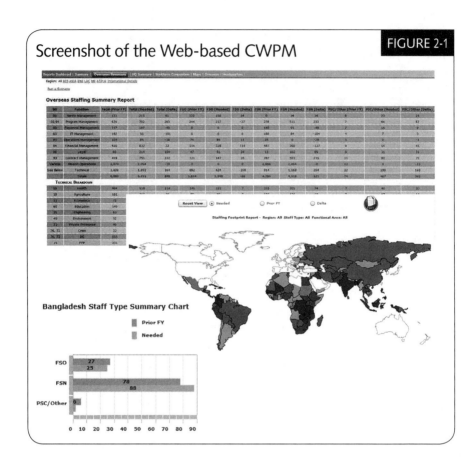

Screenshot of the Web-based CWPM — FIGURE 2-1

Backed by the steering committee, PPIM officially launched the CWPM to users outside HR in November 2010. In support of this effort, PPIM partnered with HR to develop a robust suite of supplemental communication and training materials, including a workforce planning homepage on HR's intranet, user guides, a set of frequently asked questions, and several computer-based training modules. The CWPM currently has more than 200 users from across the agency, the Department of State, and OPM.

Impact

The CWPM has become a valuable source of input into USAID's planning and budgeting processes. By rationalizing and reallocating staffing based on stated workload drivers, the model has allowed decision-makers to understand and project the potential impacts of resource, organizational, and environmental changes on staffing requirements at headquarters and in the field.

For example, the Republic of South Sudan became an independent nation on July 9, 2011, effectively putting an end to Africa's longest running civil war. When the country voted for secession, agency staff looked to the CWPM for guidance in workforce planning. After adjusting a few basic assumptions to reflect projected funding increases and the difficulty of conducting business in post-conflict states, the CWPM produced a detailed report that estimated the staffing support required to operate a mission in this newly formed nation.

USAID's Development Leadership Initiative (DLI) provides another example of how the CWPM has truly become a cornerstone of the agency's hiring and resource allocation process. USAID's FY05 human capital strategic planning process and workforce analysis identified a "lack of depth in critical core areas such as education, health, and agriculture, concluding that this was severely constraining the agency's ability to 'surge' staff in support of pre- and post-conflict programs in Iraq, other critical priority countries around the world, and other foreign policy priorities. These factors, coupled with a high percentage of USAID's workforce nearing retirement, underscored the acute need for both increased hiring and better succession planning."[1]

Backed by bipartisan support and supplemental funding, the agency launched the DLI program to address these issues, with the ultimate goal of increasing its cadre of FSO staff by 1,200 positions, effectively doubling the FSO workforce. The CWPM's results have been used to guide the recruitment, hiring, and deployment of new FSOs under this large-scale effort. Specifically, USAID has targeted its hiring toward specific occupational categories (i.e., "backstops") based on the CWPM's staffing projections to achieve the right number of staff and the optimal skill mix.

In addition to recruitment and hiring, the model serves as a valuable deployment and resource allocation tool for the agency, which is imperative in a tight budget environment. A February 2012 report to Congress indicated that USAID is at approximately 75 percent of the staffing level projected by the CWPM, indicating that USAID is not fully staffed to meet its current workload requirements. Therefore, the agency has leveraged the model to institute a "fair allocation" methodology for mission-level staffing requests and deployment determinations. For example, the deputy assistant administrator of HR tasked the agency's regional bureaus with incorporating the model's projections into their official staffing requests by doing a country-by-country allocation to the CWPM's bottom-line numbers for their respective regions. Recognizing that there weren't enough resources to staff to 100 percent of the projected workload requirement, the goal of this exercise was to "structure the market" to match supply and demand more closely.

The reality is that missions in USAID's Europe and Eurasia (E&E) region are often more attractive than Africa missions, but the staffing needs in Africa dramatically outweigh those of E&E. HR then worked with the bureaus to arrange region-by-region briefings with the State Department, which plays a key role in approving staff overseas. Ultimately, USAID used the model's projections to help justify additional positions in mission-critical countries to State.

Overall, the agency has come to view the CWPM's results as a general guideline for staffing requirements. In many cases, actual staffing requests differ from the model's projections, due to budget limitations, space considerations, security concerns, and other practical realities that every organization faces. However, over the last 10 years, USAID has successfully leveraged this strategic staffing model to develop and institute a data-driven workforce planning process, which has helped the agency accomplish the following:

- Align workforce requirements to the agency's strategic goals

- Develop a comprehensive picture of where gaps exist and identify and implement gap reduction strategies

- Make strategic decisions about organizational structure and staff deployment

- Justify staffing requests to Congress and other stakeholders, which is particularly critical in a difficult budget environment.

Why It Worked

Although USAID is a unique agency that requires a highly specialized workforce planning tool, many of the issues the agency faced in developing and institutionalizing the CWPM are similar to those that any organization would face. Similarly, the key ingredients to USAID's success apply to any organization looking to develop a data-driven workforce planning process. Four key factors contributed directly to the agency's success:

1. *Engage senior leadership.* USAID quickly recognized the importance of engaging senior leadership to establish agencywide buy-in and ensure that the CWPM's assumptions and projections remain credible. For USAID, the process of updating the model's data and interpreting its results has become an increasingly coordinated effort, as PPIM must frequently gather dozens of data points from across the agency. With support and guidance from the CWPM steering committee, PPIM has been able to create and sustain relationships with key individuals to ensure these critical data updates are received. The steering committee has also been crucial in establishing and maintaining the CWPM's credibility. By routinely communicating key changes in strategic direction and reviewing and authorizing major changes to assumptions and formulae, the committee helps ensure that the tool remains relevant and aligned with overarching agency priorities.

2. *Be clear about what a staffing model isn't.* From the beginning, USAID had a clear understanding of what the CWPM was and, equally important, what it wasn't. A common mistake in workforce modeling is treating

a model's projections as "the answer." By its very nature, a model is inaccurate because it's precisely that—a model. A staffing model's value is that it alters the starting point for the discussion. Rather than beginning a conversation by looking to current or historical configurations, the discussion begins with the allocations suggested by the forward-looking model. Managers still need to weigh the results and make staffing decisions based on other considerations; the staffing model helps frame that discussion in a clear, rational, and data-driven context that managers can understand and accept. USAID has come to view and communicate the model's results as a general guideline for where the agency should be. A staffing model does not provide the right answer; instead, it offers a reasonable starting point based on data-driven assumptions.

3. *Be transparent and flexible.* To institutionalize the tool into broader agency planning and resource allocation processes, PPIM needed to shake the "black box" stereotype by increasing transparency and making the tool accessible to a broad, non-HR audience. This would not have been possible without transitioning from the cumbersome, Excel-based tool to a more intuitive and user-friendly web-based application. The stability and accuracy provided by the online application has allowed users to understand the CWPM's assumptions more easily, navigate its robust suite of planning and scenario-building capabilities, and interpret its results more effectively.

   USAID also understood that its optimal staffing profile is a moving target because workload ebbs and flows as policies, priorities, and processes change. PPIM had the foresight to build a high level of flexibility into the web-based application. With the click of a button, users can change staffing ratios, test the impacts of various funding levels, or adjust the relative distribution of certain staff types and functions.

4. *Leverage external data sources.* A key component of the CWPM's credibility, both internal and external to

the agency, is its reliance on unbiased, external data sources. Along with many other organizations across the federal government, USAID currently relies on a legacy human resource information system (HRIS) that is imperfect at best. It is cumbersome to navigate and error-prone, and extracting data is difficult. In contrast, the CWPM's projections are tied to external predictors of workload, such as the relative ease or difficulty of doing business within a country (measured by factors such as the burden of customs procedures, investor protection indices, and the average time required to start a business); the impact of infrastructure on workload (measured by factors such as surface area, value lost due to electrical outages, and registered air transport); and the capacity for USAID's overseas programs to augment FSO staffing by hiring employees from the local workforce (measured by factors such as literacy rate, mean years of schooling, and education expenditures).

Using a Workforce Planning Model to Address Current Government Requirements

To date, USAID has leveraged the CWPM primarily to identify and address workforce gaps and allocate staffing resources rationally and effectively. However, agencies can use workforce models for a variety of purposes. For example, managers can use a model to understand and weigh the risks and benefits associated with staffing reductions, which is particularly critical in a tight budget environment. A model that ties staffing to expected outcomes and production can help managers assess the impact of staff cuts on the organization's ability to continue meeting mission requirements, offering data-driven insight into key questions such as: Can we do more with less? Do the fiscal benefits of a staffing reduction outweigh the costs due to production loss?

In addition to risk assessment, an effective model can be used to identify and implement process improvements and efficiencies. Workforce planning is an iterative process; workload and staffing ratios aren't static. Instead, they must be continually updated and refined to reflect the changing nature of how an organization operates, improving over time as additional process efficiencies are introduced. Workforce planners, who routinely study and quantify the impact of these efficiencies, are thus well-positioned to help identify and institute these process improvements across the organization.

Finally, not only do workforce planning models help managers forecast workload and staffing in terms of quantity, but they are also valuable tools for identifying and understanding staffing profiles in terms of staffing mix. Specifically, models can tie staffing to cost and other sourcing considerations (e.g., the inherently governmental nature of the work, the variability of the work, whether there is a long-term need for the function), allowing managers to evaluate various sourcing scenarios and optimize the organization's mix of contractor and direct-hire staff. In this way, a workforce planning model can help organizations answer the administration's charge to better understand and manage the inherent complexity of the federal government's multisector workforce.

Whether it's in the public or private sector, workforce planning is a critical element of success for any organization. The CWPM has helped USAID transform its human capital management from a high-risk area to one that that demonstrates that data-driven planning tools can ensure that workforce requirements align with an agency's strategic goals and budget parameters. The ability to leverage this planning tool to inform recruitment, staff placement, and agency budget planning has better positioned the agency to achieve the primary goal outlined in its human capital strategic plan: "Getting the right people in the right place, doing the right work, at the right time (with knowledge, skills and experience) to pursue U.S. national interests abroad."

NOTE

1   USAID (2012), *Report to Congress on the Development Leadership Initiative*, February 2012.Washington, DC.

Meeting a Major Staffing Challenge

Customs and Border Protection

Glenn Sutton
Mike McManus
Jenna Bender

In mid-2006, the Bush administration was determined to make substantial and visible progress in protecting U.S. borders and reducing illegal immigration. A key part of the strategy was to dramatically increase the size of the U.S. Border Patrol, a component of the Customs and Border Protection Bureau (CBP). With the administration's commitment to the public, the agency was faced with the challenge of increasing the number of border patrol agents from just over 12,000 to more than 18,000, a staffing increase of 50 percent, in just 18 months. The increase of 6,000 agents actually required more than 9,000 hires to cover projected agency attrition and dropouts during the rigorous screening process, as well as during the Border Patrol Academy training required for all new officers. CBP achieved this remarkable goal.

CBP's Staffing Challenge

Then-Assistant Commissioner for Human Resources Robert Hosenfeld likened CBP's staffing challenge to an automobile race: "We were constantly using metrics and real-time data to make adjustments, just like they do in NASCAR." The following were among the challenges Robert and his team faced:

- An HR staff that normally hired fewer than 50 new employees per month was now expected to hire more than 250 per month.

- A booming economy with low unemployment rates made locating and attracting qualified and suitable candidates difficult.

- Candidates had to be screened at several levels to determine if they met all the stringent requirements of law enforcement work, including:

  - *Basic qualifications review.* Did the candidate have experience or potential in the law enforcement area? During this time period, most graduates of law enforcement education programs were being hired by local police departments and were not interested in border patrol positions. CBP recruiters found that applicants with military and related experience were often excellent candidates for the bureau's law enforcement jobs.

  - *Security and background checks.* Candidates had to have clean backgrounds with no drug or major arrest record, and a reasonable credit history. This eliminated many candidates early in the hiring process.

  - *Logic exams.* Border patrol agents have to apply good judgment in ambiguous situations within split seconds; there is not always a standard textbook answer. This was a challenge for some groups of candidates. For example, it was discovered that many candidates from a major city with a strong manufacturing tradition found it difficult to make decisions that did not fit within a rigid set of rules; consequently, they were not viable candidates. Detailed analysis of this type of information helped CBP focus its recruiting resources in areas with a higher likelihood of success.

  - *Foreign language (Spanish) aptitude exams.* Because most of the work is along the U.S.–Mexico border, basic proficiency in Spanish was a common requirement. CBP provided Spanish language training, but candidates had to be bilingual in English and Spanish or at least have a basic aptitude and willingness to learn the second language.

○ *Physical and psychological exams.* The areas covered by border patrol agents are typically remote, and living conditions are often harsh. Significant physical demands are involved in pursuing and apprehending suspects. The exams revealed whether candidates were up to those conditions. Psychological exams were similar to those required for essentially all law-enforcement positions for which a weapon is required.

○ *Other requirements such as driving vehicles and firearms skills.* Candidates had to be able to drive and use firearms. While driving would seem to be a common ability, some candidates from major cities did not even have driver's licenses. Other candidates chose not to pursue the position once they realized that the use of firearms was a mandatory part of the job.

The CBP Mission

- CBP is the largest law enforcement agency within the Department of Homeland Security, with over 58,000 employees serving both nationwide and overseas.

- CBP's priority mission is to prevent terrorists and terrorist weapons from entering the United States and to ensure the security of our nation at its borders and ports of entry while allowing legitimate travel and trade, which are vital to our economy and way of life.

- CBP is responsible for apprehending individuals attempting to enter the United States illegally; stemming the flow of illegal drugs and other contraband; protecting our agricultural and economic interests from harmful pests and diseases; protecting American businesses from theft of their intellectual property; and regulating and facilitating international trade, collecting import duties, and enforcing U.S. trade laws.

Successful completion of a 12-week law enforcement course at the Border Patrol Academy in the middle of a New Mexico desert was one of the final requirements. This too was a source of some attrition as the staffing process reached its conclusion.

Candidates dropped out at each step of the process, mostly when the primary job criteria were applied through tests. Significant numbers fell out at the later stages of the process, even as they reported for work on their first day.

To get one hire in place at the border, CBP needed to consider approximately 30 initial applicants (Figure 3-1). This result dramatically expanded the scope of the outreach required to meet CBP's hiring targets within the limited timeframe—and this was only the first of many challenges the team had to address.

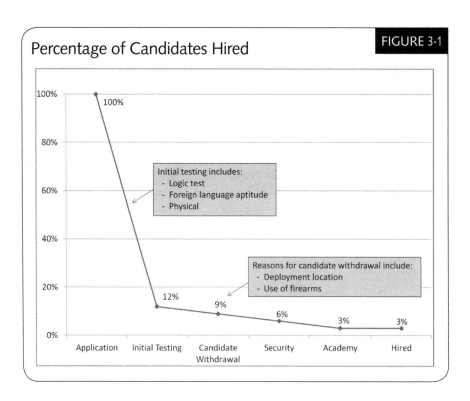

FIGURE 3-1

Percentage of Candidates Hired

Initial testing includes:
- Logic test
- Foreign language aptitude
- Physical

Reasons for candidate withdrawal include:
- Deployment location
- Use of firearms

The final staffing hurdle was the job itself, which frequently meant high-stress work assignments in harsh and austere conditions at remote sites. The attrition rate of agents once onboard ranged from 11 percent to almost 17 percent per year during the hiring surge period. Factoring in that ongoing onboard attrition, the initial staffing target of 6,000 additional agents meant that CPB had to hire well over 9,000 agents (Figure 3-2).

The numbers in Figure 3-2 reflect only border patrol agent hires and onboard strength. During this time period, CBP increased hiring for virtually all CBP functions to support the larger agent workforce, adding to the agency's significant recruitment challenge.

How did CBP even begin to plan and execute such an ambitious undertaking? Metrics were a central tool that provided the framework and a way to assess progress throughout the process—from determining the most promising hiring sources,

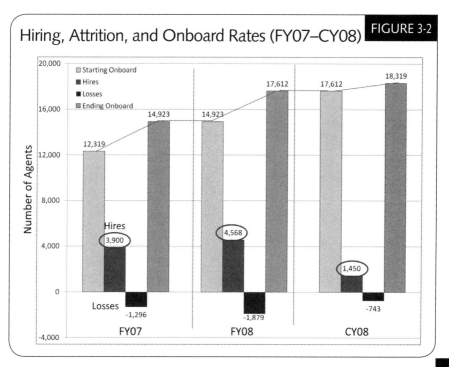

Hiring, Attrition, and Onboard Rates (FY07–CY08)   FIGURE 3-2

to factoring in attrition at various stages of recruitment, to adjusting strategies and efforts based on actual results. In fact, effective metrics provided the compelling case the team needed to get critical resources throughout the process. But first, they had to get the candidates in the door.

Beyond "Post and Pray"

Robert Hosenfeld and his team deployed a wide variety of methods to attract applicants, including the Number 28 car in NASCAR's nationwide series. Highlights include the following:

- The team used metrics and data analysis to identify candidate-rich locations for both advertising and local job fairs. They reviewed statistics such as foreclosure rates and unemployment rates by congressional district to help identify potential hiring pools.

- CBP used the internet, radio, television, movie theaters, and transit ads to communicate its brand and announce hiring opportunities and events. At major public events, CBP deployed simple technology monitors to display current activities at the southwest border. Interested applicants could submit resumes via the internet.

- The team identified candidates who had recently completed their military obligations and made contact with them at military transition centers. Veterans typically have training and experience that match up well to border agent requirements; they represented 23 percent of newly hired agents during the hiring surge. CPB also focused on college campuses to advertise to students and recruit graduates looking for work.

- CBP turned to its own border patrol agents to represent the agency and recruit at hiring events. The agents were able to provide a realistic picture of the job while sharing their passion for protecting the country. With the agents participating in simultaneous hiring events across various parts of the country, CPB typically exceeded the weekly target of 3,500 applicants, averaging over 4,500 applicants per week throughout the second half of FY2008.

- CBP created a minority recruitment strike team composed entirely of African American border patrol agents. The strike team's focus was on demonstrating that minorities are successfully involved with border patrol efforts and increasing the percentage of minorities in the CBP through direct contact and discussions with minority candidates.

- Rodeo events provided great opportunities for recruitment. Professional Bull Riders, Inc., proved to be a good partner and a useful avenue for recruitment. One of the bull riders also happened to be a CBP agent who wore his CBP chaps with pride.

- CBP recruited students and interns through a variety of programs. The CBP explorer program provided high school students with opportunities to participate in federal enforcement-related activities. The student career experience program and student temporary employment program offered opportunities for students to learn about careers at CBP and gain valuable work experience. The federal career intern program hired talent in a variety of entry-level positions in a two-year internship that could lead to permanent placement within the agency. The presidential management fellows program provided opportunities for graduate students, who often had prior experience in public administration, technology, science, health, human resources, business, and financial management. These programs are now part of the federal pathways program.

- The CBP website, www.CBP.gov, provided the full picture of CBP's mission and accomplishments. The careers section provided comprehensive information to potential applicants, including an overview of careers at CBP, the application process, study guides and preparation manuals, resume tips, and links to the central applicant self-service (CASS) system.

The NASCAR Initiative

The NASCAR nationwide series sponsorship was a multipurpose marketing and recruiting tool, enabling CBP to communicate about the Border Patrol to a nationwide audience over an extended period of time. On the track, the race car served as a rolling billboard; at trackside, CBP set up recruitment booths at the track's "midway," where fans walk around and seek entertainment before the race. In addition, several promotional events involving the car and driver took place outside the track.

The demographics of NASCAR fans indicated potential candidates, and sponsorship raised public awareness about the border patrol in several untapped markets. Each NASCAR race weekend became a recruiting opportunity either through border patrol agents conducting on-site recruiting or through word-of-mouth from others who learned about CBP through NASCAR racing.

A good example of the impact of NASCAR on recruiting occurred in Laredo, Texas, where the Jay Robinson racing team made a "pit stop" with NASCAR Monte Carlo #28 on their way to a race in Mexico City. The car was on display during an all-day recruiting event at a local shopping mall. The event drew large crowds, and local and national border patrol recruiters were on hand to answer questions and take applications. Lines formed as prospective applicants keyed in their applications on several laptops. By the time the event ended, recruiters had accepted 190 applications.

Internal Factors Required for Success

How did Robert Hosenfeld and his team overcome the obstacles to success that inevitably arise from the often-sticky internal mechanisms of any government agency? Several internal factors were instrumental in the program's success:

- *Leadership commitment and support* at the top of Border Patrol, CBP, and DHS. The President's specific and public commitment to have an agent Border Patrol force of over 18,000 by the end of calendar year 2008 established a clear priority for leadership at all levels.

- *Focused objective shared by all.* This was not just an HR recruiting task, but an objective for the whole agency. Top management supported the efforts and expressed a keen interest in getting results. Their priorities cascaded down through the organization. Border Patrol agents and supervisors were actively involved in the recruiting process, which freed the HR task group to focus on strategies and scheduling.

- *Sufficient budgetary resources.* Because the onboard target and time factors were set and could not be adjusted, the only remaining major variable was the resources that could be applied. The team effectively made the case at the outset that additional budget and resources would be required to meet the ambitious hiring targets within the limited timeframe.

- *Innovative ways to assess candidates.* CBP applied compressed processing techniques in the application and screening activities in several locations, including El Paso, San Diego, and Buffalo. They also used videos to evaluate the skills of potential officers: Applicants would participate in true-to-life scenarios taking place on a television screen while a video camera captured their reactions. Those who performed well entered the formal interview and selection process.

- *Expanded infrastructure to support the influx of hires.* The influx of new-agent recruits required a surge in training, equipment, and facilities. CBP expanded its staff and resources accordingly in support of functions such as human resources, finance, and facilities.

- *Ability to manage complex logistical arrangements.* Job fairs and hiring events took place simultaneously at multiple locations across the country.

- *Team and agency flexibility.* CBP continued to get better and faster at recruiting throughout the process.

They learned what to communicate and how to ask the critical questions up front (e.g., any arrest record?) to identify show-stoppers before the process went very far. The team reviewed lessons learned every week, made quick decisions, and took prompt actions in response to continually changing situations. Training was tailored when possible to meet specific recruiting needs and special applications (e.g., Rosetta Stone Spanish language learning tools) proved to be effective in building required language proficiency. The goal was not just to meet hiring numbers, but to provide a capable and qualified workforce.

Metrics, More Metrics, and Micro-Metrics

"As we began to plan and execute this effort, it became clear to me that we would not be able to meet the goal without real-time, detailed data on every stage of every process and sub-process involved. So, for nearly two years, I had a statistician attached at the hip." That's Robert Hosenfeld's modest summary of a tremendously successful deployment of data-driven HR leadership and process management. Here's how it worked:

- CBP used extensive databases to assess current and prior agency statistics on hires, attritions, and workforce configuration. Multiple employment-related databases were integrated to capture various statistics from numerous sources and incorporate them into meaningful presentations to keep management informed and the process on track. Data ranged from macro trends and analysis to the tracked status of every single applicant, including where applications were originating, the application flow, and dropouts at each phase. The intensive analysis of all aspects of the process in near real-time led to timely and effective adjustments in the approach and the application of resources.

- The team stepped back and looked at the big picture of the entire process, establishing inputs, assumptions, and projections. Analysts began with the required end result and worked backward through every stage to factor in the time required and dropouts at each step. From these extrapolations, which were continually adjusted with real-time data, they determined the volume of hires required at the front end to reach the ultimate onboard target.

- Because the resulting onboard strength target was set, the number of hires and time were the key variables. The quality of hires was also an important part of the process; cost became a secondary factor.

- The team applied various forms of analysis to find recruits. For example, they looked at statistics by congressional district (e.g., foreclosure rates, unemployment rates) to determine whether there was likely a viable pool of potential candidates.

- Continuous monitoring of "micro-metrics" enabled the team to assess results and progress toward the goal. CPB leadership realized that a high-level, executive dashboard view of data would not be adequate to identify and manage problems deep in the staffing process. For example, if some recruiting locations or methods were not productive (e.g., low numbers of applicants, poor candidates), strategies were adjusted immediately and resources were applied in more productive ways. Deployment of recruiting resources was adjusted in response to data coming in; the pace was fast, and so were the adjustments.

The team continuously monitored various micro-metrics, such as application rates and dropouts each month (Table 3-1).

However, the team reported only the major metric of "onboard agents against the plan" to top management—to keep their "eye on the ball" and to focus on final results (Figure 3-3).

Table 3-1. Monthly Micro-Metrics

Reporting Date	# Weekly Applicants (Weekly Goal 3,500)	Border Patrol Agent Cases to Internal Affairs	Internal Affairs Clears
3/27/2008 - 4/02/2008	4,300	260	100
4/03/2008 - 4/08/2008	4,600	190	40
4/09/2008 - 4/16/2008	5,200	170	260
4/17/2008 - 4/23/2008	6,000	400	110
4/24/2008 - 4/30/2008	4,700	410	90
. . .	. . .	. . .	. . .
9/18/2008 - 9/24/2008	3,900	410	220
Monthly Average	**4,600**	**430**	**130**

Note: Information provided depicts one type of metric analyzed. Values posted are rounded and are not specific applicant data.

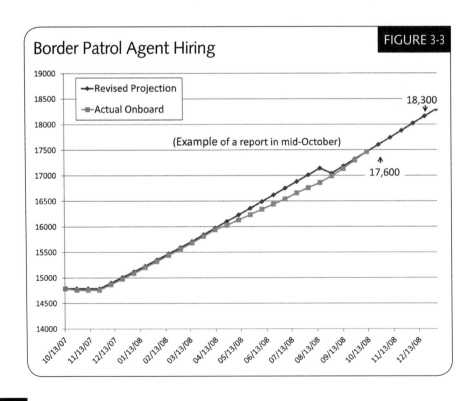

Border Patrol Agent Hiring

FIGURE 3-3

(Example of a report in mid-October)

18,300

17,600

Thanks to the innovative approaches of the team and involvement and participation across the CBP organization, the agency's formidable staffing need was exceeded, with 18,319 agents onboard by the end of calendar year 2008. This hiring surge effort not only achieved the goal, but also established a framework and process for maintaining onboard strength into the future.

Lessons Learned

CBP's staffing challenge was not accomplished without some trial and error during the 18-month duration of the initiative. The key was to analyze the ongoing data and correct course along the way. The team used data and analysis at the outset to scope out the requirements and project the number of hires that would be required. When faced with an anomaly, they immediately took action to respond. For example, when local labor markets did not have qualified candidates that fit job requirements, the team quickly moved on to other areas where data indicated a higher likelihood of success.

Robert Hosenfeld notes that four key aspects were critical to success:

- *Buy-in of the objective across the organization.* There was support and participation from top management to agents to support staff.

- *Focus on one objective.* In this case, the objective was to achieve the onboard agent target by the end of calendar year 2008.

- *Participation of the entire agency.* For example, 300 agents and three staff members were involved in a major hiring effort in Ohio.

- *Access to near real-time data and metrics.* The analysis of these data and metrics was critical in each step of the decision process to determine adjustments in resources and effort.

The CBP team had to think outside the box from traditional government hiring processes while complying with federal hiring regulations. Extraordinary actions were required to meet this daunting hiring challenge. The Border Patrol committed significant resources and manpower to achieve the goal; the HR office managed the recruitment effort through others and collaborated with colleagues (e.g., training, internal affairs, senior leadership) in an orchestrated effort to achieve the president's and the country's priorities.

Key actions included the following:

- Using metrics effectively throughout the process, from planning to adjusting course to reporting progress

- Incorporating agents into the hiring process to help meet the surge requirements and add value

- Expanding the processing and support structure to bring new hires on board and prepare them for the job

- Reaching viable candidates through creative thinking, such as NASCAR sponsorship and rodeo events

- Remaining focused and flexible to respond to ever-changing recruitment environments and situations.

While other organizations throughout the federal government may not face as daunting a hiring goal, they could benefit from many of CBP's innovative techniques. Metrics can be a powerful tool, especially when coupled with creative thinking and an unwavering focus on the key objective.

For CBP, the rigorous and innovative use of databases allowed the team to apply strategies and make decisions immediately based on the realities of the labor market and actual results. Their application of relevant data guided their decisions and provided a compelling case to leadership that won continued support throughout the process. It also defended the team's sometimes-unique approaches externally—for example, sponsoring a race car was viewed with a lot of skepticism until the resulting data clearly demonstrated the positive impact on recruitment. In summary, effective use of data coupled with creative thinking led to the unwavering commitment of leadership and the ultimate success of the CBP recruitment challenge.

Strategically Integrating New Employees

4

National Science Foundation
Center for Veterinary Medicine

Maggie Moore
Jessica Dzieweczynski
Jessica Milloy
Danny McGeehan

What do you remember about your first day on the job? You likely had a lot of questions about your role and responsibilities in your new organization: What should I be doing today? My first month? By the end of my first six months? You probably also had questions about office logistics and operations: How do I log into my email? Where's the printer? Other questions are more informal in nature, and perhaps you didn't feel there was anybody you could ask directly: Where and when should I eat lunch? Can I drop by someone's office if I have a question or should I send a meeting request? What does the office dress code really mean?

Walking into your first day on the job can be an intimidating experience. First impressions are important—for both the new employee and the organization. All too often, employees arrive on their first day to find an empty desk or an improperly functioning computer, a manager who is unaware of their start date, or simply a big pile of intimidating paperwork. How an organization handles this first experience sets the tone for the relationship, can leave a lasting impression on the employee's productivity and satisfaction, and often has an impact on whether the employee decides to stay with the organization.

Onboarding refers to the process of strategically integrating new employees into the organization's culture and their specific position. An effective onboarding process provides new employees with a range of tools, resources, and connections they need to succeed on the job. All organizations have a basic orientation process, most likely involving the completion of HR forms and ensuring that employees have basic resources (e.g., desk, computer) to perform their job. Many organizations go a step further by providing a handbook or orientation session that covers topics related to company history, culture, policies, and procedures. The most strategic organizations take a more comprehensive approach to acclimating employees by implementing an onboarding process that begins as soon as an employment offer is accepted and extends throughout the first year of employment (Table 4-1).

Table 4-1. Orientation vs. Onboarding

Orientation	Onboarding
Typically less than one week	Continuous
Owned and executed by HR	Integrates multiple offices and functions
Addresses some new employee needs	Addresses most new employee needs
Employee attends	Employee is active participant
Yields completed paperwork and general information	Maximizes employee engagement and retention

But at a time when many organizations are facing reduced training and travel budgets, does it make sense to invest those precious resources in onboarding? Consider these numbers: Each year, about 25 percent of the working population in the United States experience a career transition.[1] Over 85 percent of new employees decide whether to stay with the organization within their first six months on the job.[2] Approximately 50 percent of externally hired senior employees fail within the first 18 months in the new job.[3] Transitions like these are not cheap: In 2011, the National Association of Colleges and Employers (NACE) reported the average cost-per-hire at $5,054.[4] Executives hired through external search firms are no exception to this high cost and in fact can cost considerably more than the average cost-per-hire.

While the costs of hiring and the loss of productivity are easy to calculate, the more intangible impacts of a new hire's time to productivity or turnover (particularly for a leadership position) can have a rippling effect on the organization in terms of workload, employee morale, and leadership vision. With so many individuals entering new positions—and many of them quickly failing or choosing to leave—it simply makes sense to invest in onboarding new hires through a thoughtful and strategic process. Organizations that choose to invest in comprehensive onboarding processes are rewarded with a range of positive outcomes, including improved performance, increased engagement, and decreased turnover.

While onboarding processes vary greatly depending on the position, organization, and available resources, a comprehensive onboarding program integrates the "4 Cs": compliance, clarification, culture, and connection:[5]

- *Compliance* refers to teaching new employees about the basic rules and regulations that govern the work environment, such as applicable laws, personnel regulations, and organizational rules.

- *Clarification* involves assimilating new employees into their specific positions, including roles, responsibilities, and associated expectations.

- *Culture* refers to orienting new employees not only to formal processes but also to informal organizational norms, values, and cultural aspects that have an impact on "how we get things done around here."

- *Connection* refers to facilitating interpersonal relationships that will help employees perform.

What form the "4 Cs" take in an organization's onboarding process—and which elements are stressed—will depend on the specific needs of the population. For example, demonstrating and reinforcing the organizational culture may be particularly important for geographically dispersed organizations where a new employee may become more familiar with the local sub-culture than with overarching organizational values. Similarly, strong networks are particularly important for individuals in leadership-level positions; accordingly, an onboarding program aimed at this population should provide ample opportunity and resources for connection.

The Case of the National Science Foundation

At one point or another, turnover is a fact of life for every organization. But imagine the challenges that arise when turnover is ingrained in your business model. Such is the case with the National Science Foundation (NSF), where approximately 15 percent of the workforce are in short-term "rotator" positions. Many of these individuals are top researchers from academic institutions who come to NSF for a brief period (one to four years) to apply their knowledge related to a particular scientific field. While this model brings the latest scientific knowledge and a wealth of innovative ideas to NSF—which is critical to the progress of science and engineering fields—it requires the continual onboarding of new employees. Moreover, because most rotating personnel come to NSF from an academic environment with culture and processes that differ dramatically from those of a federal agency, the need to orient new employees to the work environment and federal frameworks within which NSF operates becomes even more pressing.

Recognizing these needs as a business imperative, NSF undertook a series of efforts to revamp its process for onboarding its general workforce and to develop a robust onboarding program specifically targeted at its executive workforce. NSF's eventual success in onboarding its workforce came largely from its emphasis on making new employee assimilation an integrated, ongoing process rather than a single event. At its core, NSF's onboarding programs address the wide array of new employee needs—from knowing what to expect before their first day, to understanding the specific culture and work practices of their individual division and job function, to transferring critical knowledge from a departing executive to an incoming leader.

Through the implementation of blended, phased activities starting before day one and continuing through year one, NSF arms new hires with an array of resources that enable them to take an active role in their own onboarding. At the same time, NSF focuses on providing guidance and tools to supervisors, administrative staff, HR professionals, and other participants involved in supporting new employee assimilation—in effect making new employee onboarding central to everyone's job.

Compliance

In accord with federal legal and organizational security requirements, a new employee's first experience includes a slew of paperwork and numerous compliance-driven activities. Is there any good way to communicate the laundry list of rules, regulations, and responsibilities the typical employee must understand and accept within the first eight hours on the job? With a little foresight and the help of technology, organizations can make even the most paperwork-intensive requirements seem painless.

One objective of NSF's New Employee Welcome (NEW) program is to do just that. Starting with an individual's acceptance of a job, the Division of Human Resources (HRM) sends the new employee a comprehensive package of materials, including an invitation to visit the NEW website, where he or she can access information about NSF's mission, history, and organizational structure as well as learn about benefits and career-life programs (Figure 4-1). This self-service portal helps employees come prepared for their first day knowing both what to expect and what to bring. All new employees are provided contact information for an HRM representative, who contacts them directly prior to their arrival to welcome them to NSF and answer

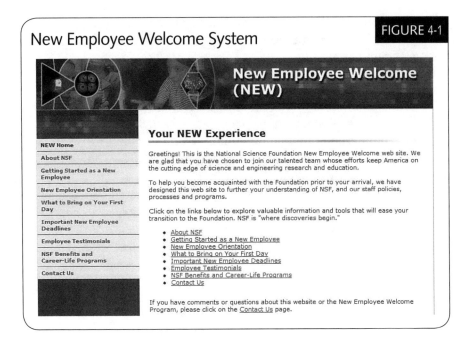

any questions they may have about their first day (e.g., logistics, transportation).

Employees then begin their first day in NSF's New Employee Orientation (NEO) program. Depending on an employee's specific job and employment arrangement, he or she may attend one or two days of orientation addressing topics ranging from conflicts of interest to available learning and development opportunities. Scheduling is flexible and is tailored by employment type. All employees view a video about NSF's mission, including perspectives from current staff about what it is like to work at NSF, which provides a consistent preview to all new hires.

To address organization-specific onboarding requirements, NSF maintains a comprehensive resource for welcoming new employees on its internal website. Since supervisors and staff don't always know the best way to become involved in onboarding and supporting new employees, the website provides an overview of the welcome process and detailed guidance for supervisors, administrative staff, and liaisons ("buddies"). Program guides, checklists of activities, sample communications and talking points, and frequently asked questions make it easy for a range of players to support the onboarding process.

In addition to the NEW program, which is geared to the needs of the general workforce, NSF designed and implemented an onboarding program tailored specifically to new executives. The new executive transition (NExT) program supports transitions into NSF executive positions from within NSF, other federal agencies, and outside the government. The program aims to support executives in reaching full performance as quickly as possible by developing knowledge about NSF's mission, culture, organization, people, and business processes. To do so, NSF implemented a range of innovative tools and support systems that cover, and even go beyond, the "4 Cs" (Figure 4-2).

NExT

NSF's NExT program is widely recognized across government as a successful program and critical tool for managing leadership transitions and developing the executive corps. The U.S. Office of Personnel Management cited NExT as a model onboarding program in its 2011 report, *Hit the Ground Running: Establishing a Model Executive Onboarding Program.* The NExT program was also recognized in NSF's 2011 strategic plan as a priority for achieving management excellence.

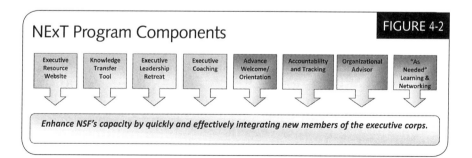

NExT Program Components   FIGURE 4-2

| Executive Resource Website | Knowledge Transfer Tool | Executive Leadership Retreat | Executive Coaching | Advance Welcome/ Orientation | Accountability and Tracking | Organizational Advisor | "As Needed" Learning & Networking |

Enhance NSF's capacity by quickly and effectively integrating new members of the executive corps.

Clarification

One of the major challenges individuals face when joining NSF's executive corps is the increase in management responsibilities compared to their jobs in academia. While new executives may have some experience managing research programs and graduate students at their university, they typically do not have experience managing the large staffs, budgets, structured performance requirements, and federal and international partnerships that contribute to NSF's mission. To help executives understand their management responsibilities, NSF developed a website that delivers critical information related to each of these areas. The *Executive Resources* website provides information on management topics ranging from managing people (e.g., how to develop performance plans, give feedback, and provide recognition) to managing scientific and administrative programs, understanding the federal budget process, and interacting with the media and international partners. Each section of the site explains an executive's role in these processes and includes tailored content and guidance specific to that role.

Recognizing that new executives tend to have little time to devote to reading lengthy guides, NSF crafted the website content to be concise, focusing on the main points of the topic and the executive's role, and providing links to more in-depth information (Figure 4-3). Each section includes a "key points" box at the top of the page, which highlights the three to five most important messages or potential landmines related to that topic and provides a point of contact for questions and additional information.

New executives also need to be oriented to the information and processes of their individual organization, such as their division's budget, personnel, and scientific programs. The tenures of the departing and the incoming executives often do not overlap, contributing to the high potential for critical knowledge to be lost with each successive rotation. To help mitigate this issue, NSF developed and pilot-tested an automated knowledge management portal to transition key information from the departing executive to the incoming executive. The tool provides much

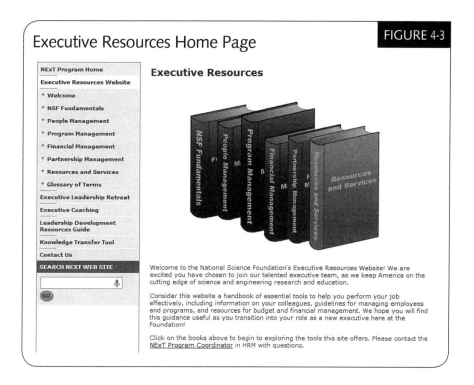

FIGURE 4-3

Executive Resources Home Page

of the same information as the website—key contacts, projects and collaborations, budget, personnel, program management— but offers an insider's perspective on these processes by allowing the departing executive to leave notes and key files for the new executive. Similar to the traditional letter an outgoing president leaves for his successor, this tool facilitates a transition "brain dump."

Culture

Individuals joining NSF from an academic institution are typically entering an organizational culture that is quite different for them. To help acclimate executives to its unique culture, NSF holds a semiannual three-day executive leadership retreat. The discussion-based agenda focuses heavily on NSF culture, using both small and large group discussions to facilitate understanding the challenges and opportunities of working effectively within NSF's organizational culture.

During the retreat, experienced NSF executives (called retreat "resource advisors") lead discussions, ask direct questions, and share lessons learned. The participants also gain insight into important organizational dynamics, such as interacting with external stakeholders and effectively leading other scientists. Finally, several self-assessments are conducted, including a 360-degree feedback tool, to build self-awareness and enable leaders to reflect on opportunities to develop their weaknesses and leverage their strengths within the NSF environment.

Connection

Networking—and having the right connections—is an essential component of being an effective leader. Several components of the NExT program facilitate critical contacts and relationships. For example, networking is a core focus of the executive leadership retreat, which facilitates connection through small group discussions as well as more formal "speed networking" activities. Retreat participants consistently report that making connections is one of the most useful aspects of the retreat.

In addition, NSF designed and implemented leadership networking events that are conducted twice a year, on alternate quarters from the leadership retreat. This ensures that all executives have an opportunity to meet and connect with their colleagues within three months of joining the organization. Because the entire tenure of a rotating executive is only two years, facilitating connections quickly is important for success.

Additional Support for Executives

In addition to components targeting the "4 Cs," NSF recognized the importance of providing resources to address the specific challenges that many executives face. NSF implemented an executive coaching program in which a qualified, external

Connecting Long Distance

Many organizations face the same challenges of helping new hires connect with colleagues and peers, but with the added complication of needing to connect across distances greater than a hallway. One such organization, the Commercial Services Program (CSP) of the National Park Service (NPS), figured out how to crack that nut and connect employees located in some of the most diverse work locations imaginable.

CSP consists of approximately 300 full-time and collateral-duty employees geographically dispersed across the continental United States as well as Alaska, Hawaii, and Puerto Rico, and at various organizational levels (headquarters support offices, eight regional offices, and nearly 120 parks). Yet, the challenges facing new hires are not all that different from those facing any new hires: becoming part of a community, having the right resources on hand to be productive, and having a common, consistent onboarding experience. The variety of locations requires a more creative approach to ensure that onboarding happens just as effectively for a new hire at the Grand Canyon as for a new hire located in the middle of the national mall. Some employees may be the only person in their park performing these duties, with no one nearby to turn to with questions and for guidance. Further, given limited travel funding, it might be months before a new hire is able to meet with another CSP employee in person at a training event or conference. After employees at all levels noted that this isolation was particularly detrimental to the onboarding process, NPS decided to think about relationship building in a more virtual environment.

In addition to the traditional onboarding tools that can be distributed via a robust SharePoint site (e.g., a self-guided orientation presentation, key points of contact, tip sheets to help with common duties), NPS decided to build a strong buddy program. Like traditional programs, CSP's buddy program matches a more tenured peer to a new hire to help integrate the new hire into the organization and understand the informal norms and culture. Unlike other organizations with colocated employees, this program is largely reliant on email, phone, and SharePoint. These technologies bridge the geographical distances between the buddies. Building these relationships allows new hires the opportunity to jumpstart their networking across the organization well before they are able to attend a workshop or training. In addition to communicating the unwritten rules of culture, buddies also open their professional networks to the new hires and make introductions on their behalf (also virtually), particularly to connect the new hire with individuals at parks with similar operations.

This low-cost component can have a significant impact on a new hire's success in an environment where there may not be anyone nearby to ask for advice or guidance. It also demonstrates that having someone "just a phone call away" can be as effective as having someone upstairs or around the corner.

coach is paired with a new or seasoned executive to equip the executive with the tools, knowledge, and opportunities needed for self-development, personal growth, and enhanced work effectiveness. The coach helps the executive talk through specific challenges he or she is facing and develop and practice skills to help him or her face those challenges and generally be more effective. The learning that takes place in individual coaching sessions is reinforced through structured coaching program activities, including a monthly article that focuses on a common challenge and bimonthly brown bags that provide executives an opportunity to share lessons learned with their colleagues. The articles and brown bags have covered topics such as dealing with uncertainty (specifically in the current federal climate), delegation, and emotional intelligence. These activities help expand the reach and impact of individual coaching engagements to groups of executives who are likely facing similar challenges.

The Importance of Evaluation

Results are useful only if they can be measured and assessed through an evaluation process. Ultimately, an onboarding program should have a measurable impact on both individual and organizational performance. To that end, the evaluation of a program should be focused not only on general employee feedback, effectiveness, and efficiency, but also on the organizational need it was designed to address (e.g., retention, engagement, time to productivity).

NSF continually conducts evaluation activities for each of the NExT components, providing input on how to adapt components to meet shifting needs and demonstrating the program's impact on leadership effectiveness. For example, evaluation statistics indicate that 100 percent of coaching participants (1) learned skills they can use on the job, (2) believe the coaching program made them more effective as an NSF executive, and (3) would recommend the program to other executives. Similarly, approximately 90 percent of leadership retreat

Participant Perspectives

Coaching Program

"This [coaching program] was particularly valuable in a time of transition in my career at NSF. I needed to learn a new culture, and talking it through was important."

Leadership Retreat

"Very educational – I learned how certain things are done at NSF that I had not previously known."

"The peer-to-peer interaction helped me in the development of my executive network."

participants expect to use what they learned from the retreat and will recommend the retreat to others. Statistics such as these, along with anecdotal evidence from participants, help demonstrate NSF's return on its investment in onboarding new employees.

Measuring Success at the Center for Veterinary Medicine

Constant evaluation is a crucial aspect of maintaining an onboarding program that is both effective and engaging for new employees. The Food and Drug Administration's Center for Veterinary Medicine (CVM), currently 500 employees strong, is in charge of regulating the manufacturing and distribution of food additives and drugs for animals. Given the highly specialized nature of the scientific positions at CVM, it is essential to familiarize new employees with their roles as quickly as possible. To meet this need, CVM has developed a comprehensive onboarding program that begins weeks before the new hire starts work and continues through his or her first year.

CVM's human capital management staff realize that the program will remain effective only as long as new employees stay engaged throughout the process. To this end, CVM continually evaluates the program through a series of surveys and focus groups. Engagement and effectiveness are measured using a trio of surveys taken at different phases throughout a new employee's first year. Each survey measures a specific aspect of the onboarding program:

- Entrance survey. The CVM entrance survey which is given to new employees a month after hire, focuses on the hiring process, welcome packet, and their first four weeks.

- Integration survey. The CVM integration survey, which is given to new employees as well as their hosts (i.e., "buddies") 90 days after hire, examines the CVM's buddy program as well as both parties' general feelings about the onboarding process and activities.

- Overall onboarding evaluation survey. The CVM overall onboarding evaluation survey is given to new employees on their one-year anniversary. This survey addresses the employee's current level of engagement, evaluates the effectiveness of work processes, and allows the employee to rate his or her interest in continuing employment with CVM.

Surveys are an essential part of CVM's evaluation process, providing employees an anonymous way to critique the program as well as a formalized means to request program additions or changes. New employee survey feedback has already spurred the creation of a streamlined orientation session. Survey data showed that new employees were overwhelmed by the six-hour orientation sessions, so CVM reduced the sessions to two hours, focusing on the key question, "How do I fit into this organization?" New employees gain a firm understanding of why they were hired and how they will contribute to CVM's mission.

CVM also balances the quantitative data provided by surveys with focus groups for new employees and other staff members involved in the onboarding process. These focus groups help create the lively dialogue that surveys simply cannot, and have resulted in a number of improvements to the onboarding program. For example, a common theme throughout many onboarding focus groups was that new employees would benefit from more interaction with each other throughout their first year. CVM was able to meet this request by facilitating on-boarding roundtable discussions. These discussions, which now take place twice a year, allow new employees to discuss their experiences with other recent hires.

CVM's human capital management staff also takes an active role in bolstering the onboarding program by keeping new employee resources up-to-date and ensuring that public and private best practices are considered when revising the program. The new employee welcome packet and webpage are updated every three months, with an eye to what other government agencies and private sector organizations are doing.

By combining a variety of evaluation strategies, CVM is able to lead the way in onboarding and remains a best practice program within both its parent department and government as a whole.

The Bottom Line

Over 85 percent of new employees decide whether to stay with an organization within their first six months on the job;[6] on average, it takes new executives a minimum of six months to become fully productive in their role.[7] Strategically implementing an onboarding program that engages employees early and speeds time to productivity just makes sense; it is one of the most basic and cost-effective means to maximize employee productivity and retention. The onboarding programs at NSF and CVM have had measurable positive impacts; they provide a blueprint for other organizations to model in developing, implementing, and evaluating general and targeted onboarding programs.

While many components of an onboarding program can be universally applied (e.g., timeline, welcome packet, buddy program), the unique needs and culture of the organization should be reflected in the program design. A strong onboarding program is one of the best first impressions your organization can make; having happy, productive new hires is always an investment worth making.

NOTES

1   K. Rollag, S. Parise, and R. Cross (2005), "Getting New Hires Up to Speed Quickly." *MIT Sloan Management Review* 46, 35–41.

2   *All Aboard: Effective Onboarding Techniques and Strategies* (2008). Aberdeen Group, Boston, MA.

3   B. Smart (1999),*Topgrading: How Leading Companies Win by Hiring, Coaching, and Keeping the Best People.* Upper Saddle River, NJ: Prentice Hall.

4   *2011 Recruiting Benchmarks Survey* (2011). National Association of Colleges and Employers, Bethlehem, PA.

5   T.N. Bauer (2010), *Onboarding New Employees: Maximizing Success.* SHRM Foundation, Alexandria, VA.

6   *All Aboard: Effective Onboarding Techniques and Strategies* (2008). Aberdeen Group, Boston, MA.

7   M. Moore (2008). *Spotlight on Executive Onboarding.* American Society for Public Administration, p. 5.

Innovative Recruitment and Retention

U.S. Department of Veterans Affairs

Tim Barnhart
Mike McManus

The Department of Veterans Affairs (VA) is dedicated to caring for our country's veterans in recognition of the immense sacrifices they have made for our country. With the economy struggling, many veterans face major challenges transitioning to civilian life. To help address this issue, VA launched an innovative program called VA for Vets, which officially began on Veterans Day 11/11/11. The original announcement from Eric K. Shinseki, Secretary of Veterans Affairs, noted that "VA for Vets is a high-tech and high-touch approach to recruiting, hiring, and reintegrating veterans into the VA workforce."

VA for Vets is managed by the newly created Veteran Employment Services Office (VESO). The program introduces a suite of tools and services designed to aid VA in expanding its recruitment and hiring of veterans and improving its success in retaining veterans and transitioning them into productive employment. After its initial successes, VA is now expanding the scope of the program beyond VA to promote employment of veterans across the federal government and in the nonprofit sector. Many of the strategies and tools used by VA for Vets have also proven their value as broadly applicable human capital practices transferrable to any organization seeking to improve employee recruitment and retention results. VA for Vets represents a best practice with the potential to help both federal and private organizations meet their human capital goals.

The Veteran Employment Challenge

In recent years, with the influx of veterans from Iraq and Afghanistan and a lagging economy, the veteran population has been struggling with unemployment and underemployment. A presidential mandate (Executive Order 13518) was issued to increase federal hiring of veterans and actively support their recruitment and preparation for civil service. The VA secretary created VESO and the VA for Vets program to address recruitment, retention, and reintegration of veterans into the workforce. In 2009, veterans made up 29 percent of VA's workforce; the secretary set a goal of 40 percent.

Awards Won by VA for Vets

- Human Capital Management for Defense Award for "Most Innovative Recruitment Program" and "Best Implementation of an Enterprise Technology System"
- Web Marketing Association Award for "Best Employment Online Video," "Best Government Online Video," and "Best Government Online Ad"
- 2012 Telly Award for "Best Recruitment Video"
- Human Resources Association of Greater Washington Leadership Award

To achieve the secretary's goals, VA recognized that a transformation was needed in the way it recruited and hired veterans and reintegrated them into the civilian workforce. VA for Vets is helping transform veteran recruitment and placement. The key themes driving the transformation are advocacy, empowerment, and making veterans career-ready. With these principles in mind, VESO reviewed and addressed key issues and barriers in the areas of recruitment and outreach, retention, hiring-process improvement, and reintegration. The result is a comprehensive website, with supporting services, that reaches veterans in the job market, helps them understand how their military experience relates to the market, supports them in seeking employment opportunities, and aids hiring managers in drawing on the immense talent pool of veterans to fill their vacancies.

VA for Vets includes several innovative, high-impact components:

- Virtual job fairs
- Career coaching
- Training
- Hiring process reforms
- Civilian credentialing.

Virtual Job Fairs: VA for Vets Career Center

While traditional "brick and mortar" job fairs have proven very successful, they require substantial resources to plan and operate. VESO has developed a parallel option to supplement and even replace costly job fairs. The VA for Vets career center, located on the VA for Vets website, provides an efficient, automated way to register veterans. The suite of online tools at the VA for Vets online career center website includes an advanced integrated military skills translator and career assessment tool, a resume builder, and a job search engine. Career counselors are available online or in person to assist veterans with every aspect of recruitment and reintegration into the civilian workforce.

In the first two weeks, more than 31,000 veterans visited the website, more than 3,700 registered accounts, and more than 1,900 saved resumes to the site. The coaches, veteran representatives, and help desk technicians work from two veteran coaching call centers in Dumfries, Virginia, and Edensberg, Pennsylvania, as well as a help desk facility in New Orleans, Louisiana. The website and centers provide an efficient way for veterans to register for jobs and receive the tools and counseling they need to become more marketable in the civilian sector. This comprehensive approach has made VESO's VA for Vets website the backbone of VA's hiring effort.

The following are the key components of the site (Figure 5-1):

- *Military skills translator*. A major challenge of the recruitment process, in any environment, is effectively

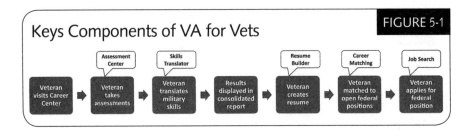

Keys Components of VA for Vets — FIGURE 5-1

communicating the candidate's skills and abilities to the potential employer. For veterans, this can be especially challenging, as they sometimes have difficulty translating military experience and terminology into civilian workplace terms. To address this challenge, VESO developed a robust military skills translator, which uses military terminology such as *service*, *rank*, and *military occupational specialty* to identify skills relevant to the civilian labor market. With further assistance from VESO staff or career coaches, the veteran candidate is automatically directed to potential civilian employment opportunities based on military experience.

- *Assessment center.* The assessment center includes a suite of online tools to aid veterans in assessing their personal interests, job-related skills, work activities, and general aptitude to help find matches with occupations available in VA and across government. The assessment center includes lengthy inventories of skills and work activities required by a broad spectrum of occupations. These, along with specially developed interest and aptitude assessment instruments, support veterans in understanding their strengths and figuring out where to target their employment search. The results of the assessment flow directly into the resume builder so they are accurately and prominently represented to hiring managers.

- *Resume builder.* Users can integrate their translated skills, assessment results, and employment history into a resume through the VA for Vets career center resume builder. The resume builder enables veterans to create resumes that provide all the information needed by government agencies. It automatically integrates results from the translator and the assessment tools, and it also provides help with resume-writing techniques. Users can maintain several versions of their resume and upload them to the VA for Vets resume database for VA hiring managers and supervisors to view.

Career Coaching

VA for Vets also provides coaching services to veterans in a variety of formats, including face-to-face, by telephone, and virtually through an online collaboration workspace. Coaches focus on providing the following support:

- Guidance on using the career center and other resources

- Application, resume, and cover letter reviews

- Practice interviews

- Follow-up support to keep job seekers on track to reach their career goals.

Virtual collaboration provides a forum for engaging and productive conversations between veterans and their coaches. Using technology that is ideally suited to online collaboration, veterans and deployed military service members can efficiently conduct professional and personal activities and work toward achieving better vocational outcomes. The live, interactive, virtual workspace provides all the benefits of an in-person meeting, yet it allows users to be anywhere in the world. Users can invite coaches, supervisors, and HR professionals to join them in their personalized, virtual room to review and edit documents, work on whiteboards, take web-based training, and more. The space also allows and encourages users to provide a personal touch by creating a personal avatar, posting photos, and sharing hobbies and interests.

Training

VA for Vets has invested in a suite of training and educational resources to help military service members, supervisors, and HR professionals prepare for and manage military deployments, including the transition back to the civilian workfoce. Through the VA for Vets site, users can access webcasts that address the entire deployment lifecycle. The following webcasts are currently available on the site:

- *Employment and Readiness.* Demonstrates effective communication between a supervisor and a military service member who has just learned of an upcoming deployment. The video includes instructions for supervisors on how to use a letter of agreement and a transition plan to clarify roles during this phase of the deployment lifecycle.

- *Predeployment 1 and 2.* Addresses the predeployment phase of the deployment lifecycle, which begins when a military service member receives orders to deploy. The training helps a supervisor use effective communications skills to address the service member's concerns while planning for the workload transition required for deployment.

- *Reintegration 1 and 2.* Helps supervisors communicate with and help a military service member transition back into a work setting after deployment. The webcast demonstrates how a supervisor can provide feedback to a military service member who has recently returned from deployment, while respecting privacy and directing the service member to additional resources that can assist with overall well-being in addition to work performance.

- *Leading the Way.* Demonstrates how supervisors and colleagues can help military service members return from deployment and adjust to the civilian workforce.

Hiring Process Reforms

The process for filling a job in the federal government is notoriously slow. President Obama recently called attention to this issue by launching an end-to-end hiring reform initiative aimed at identifying inefficiencies and obstacles in the current process and speeding up the time to hire. The end-to-end hiring initiative reduced the average time to fill a federal job from 120 days to fewer than 100 days, and a target was set for all agencies to reduce the time further to fewer than 80 days.

By contrast, VESO has demonstrated the consistent ability to fill federal government jobs through its database of veteran candidates in fewer than 25 days. VESO was successful in streamlining the rules governing the hiring of veterans by fully using special appointing authorities that enabled hiring managers to bypass certain competitive requirements when hiring veterans. Hiring managers are able to fill positions quickly with highly qualified veteran applicants.

Civilian Credentialing

One of the barriers to veterans securing civilian employment is often their lack of formally recognized credentials or certifications, despite their having extensive military experience in the fields for which the credentials are required. VESO has supported several new programs to provide job credentialing for service members leaving the military. Once they have secured the proper civilian credentials, veterans are better positioned to find the jobs that fit their skills and experience.

For example, VESO has partnered with the Veterans Health Administration (VHA) on a one-year pilot program that offers intermediate care technician (ICT) positions to separating or recently separated medics, medical technicians, and corpsmen. ICTs perform technical health care procedures under the supervision of emergency department physicians. VHA has leveraged VESO's expertise in special hiring authorities to fill ICT positions in 15 medical centers across the country.

VESO is also working closely with the Departments of Transportation and Labor to enable veterans to convert their military training and job specialty skills to careers in the transportation industry. This effort will help veterans transfer their military certifications directly to the equivalent civilian certifications and licenses.

Results and Implications

Since VESO was launched on Veterans Day, 11/11/11, it has had a powerful impact on veteran recruitment, retention, and reintegration. Hundreds of thousands of veterans have visited the VA for Vets website. VESO has received positive responses from job seekers and potential employers. The time to hire veterans has consistently been below the governmentwide competitive hiring average, and hundreds of veterans have been hired nationwide. VESO has linked veteran candidates not only to jobs in VA but to positions ranging from border patrol agents in the Customs and Border Protection Bureau to scientists at the National Science Foundation. The overall program, as well as specific components of the program, have been recognized inside and outside government, winning awards across a variety of categories, including the most innovative recruitment program, best recruitment video, and excellence in human resources.

Although VA for Vets was created with a singular focus on veterans, its success has implications that go far beyond veterans and suggests a number of best practices that would benefit any HR organization. Three notable accomplishments could be especially useful in almost any HR or organizational environment:

- *Targeted recruitment.* VA for Vets is best understood as a soup-to-nuts effort to target a particular segment of the labor market and improve recruitment and retention results for that segment. Many businesses and government organizations are also targeting veterans. In addition, organizations outside VA may also be targeting minority groups, women, people with special technical disciplines, or other labor market segments.

VA for Vets demonstrates how to target effectively—from the sophisticated suite of online tools in the career center that make the employment process easy and exciting for veterans, to the personalized attention applicants receive from coaches, to the understanding of the world of veterans that is conveyed through programs like veterans as mentors, to being fast and responsive with hiring processes that don't keep applicants waiting interminably for a decision. Any organization seeking to connect with a particular segment of the labor market would do well to study what VA for Vets has accomplished.

- *Applicant pools*. VESO has achieved great results in shortening the time to hire through the VA for Vets program. The program's success is largely attributable to the strategy of developing a standing database of qualified applicants and keeping it current and relevant to job vacancies. Although this technique is not new, VA for Vets demonstrates the impact that doing it well can have on hiring process efficiency. VA for Vets is a well-designed website that engages applicants and provides tools to help them develop relevant and valid job qualifications data that provide a solid basis for sound job matches.

- *Virtual tools and processes*. The HR profession overall has been struggling, through fits and starts, to enter the automated era. VA for Vets represents a live case study in how to make that transition effectively. While the program includes many components, its heart and soul is the website. The website draws veterans in and keeps them there throughout their employment search and even afterwards, as they begin to learn about and adapt to the VA organization. It makes the hiring process easy and efficient for hiring managers and HR professionals. It integrates all the other components of the program and creates the "high-tech, high-touch" feel that Secretary Shinseki originally envisioned when he launched the program. The way VA for Vets applies technology to a broad audience but with an individual focus offers many valuable lessons for any HR organization.

The success of this program can be attributed to several key factors:

- *Top leadership commitment.* From the start, this program has had the highest level of support, including the secretary of VA, and has benefited from its alignment with the goals and direction of the president. This support has been critical to VESO's ability to marshal the resources necessary to make the program a success. It has also been instrumental in creating enthusiasm and confidence within VA and among veterans that the federal government has a serious commitment to improved engagement of veterans.

- *Commitment at all levels.* Top-level support was effectively communicated and translated into support up and down the organization, from the HR community in VA to line hiring managers who were critical users of the program and its processes.

- *Effective application of technology.* Technology tools have made the program a success. VESO and its extended technology team built a site that worked, was integrated, and "caught on" with the user population.

- *High-touch approach.* Too often technology diminishes the quality of the customer interaction, creating frustration and resistance as users miss interacting with a real person. VESO was able to strengthen the user interaction through its technology, heightening it through the integration of additional "human" services (coaches, veteran representatives, help desk technicians, and VESO staff). The high-touch vision was successfully realized.

- *Systemic focus.* Key to the success of this program has been VESO's relentless focus on the broader issue of hiring and retaining veterans and its determination to find solutions. VESO is now looking beyond VA and even the federal government to create a larger employment market that can serve veterans better. VESO's eagerness to go wherever necessary to have maximum impact was a critical ingredient in the success of this program.

VESO's VA for Vets program has provided a comprehensive approach for VA to address employment challenges for veterans within VA, across the federal government, and throughout the nonprofit sector.

> VESO's VA for Vets program is a cornerstone initiative for VA that reflects a transformation in the way the agency recruits, retains, and reintegrates veterans. Its impact now reaches beyond VA as recruitment efforts have been extended to other federal and nonprofit organizations. It also demonstrates the effectiveness of many HR strategies and techniques that are broadly applicable.

Telework: Rethinking the Process of Work

U.S. Patent and Trademark Office

Tim Barnhart
Sherean Miller

The next time you're in Alexandria, Virginia, turn onto Dulany Street and make your way south into the heart of a beautiful, modern campus centered around the Madison building—a sleek steel and glass structure with an eye-catching ten-story atrium visible from miles around. The campus fans out to include four adjacent buildings situated among small parks, quiet traffic circles, restaurants, coffee shops, and a variety of retail stores. Old Town Alexandria, with its colonial charm, is a short walk from the King Street or Eisenhower Metro stations connecting individuals with much of the Washington, DC, metropolitan area.

The campus of the United States Patent and Trademark Office (USPTO), a component of the Department of Commerce, employs more than 10,000 patent examiners, attorneys, and other professional and administrative staff. But nearly 7,000 of its 10,000 employees don't always work there; instead, they telework from home or from an alternate worksite. Why they telework and why USPTO encourages them to do so is a long story. But if you were on the USPTO campus and looked to the south, you would quickly see one major reason: the Capital Beltway. In 2011, the Washington, DC, area was ranked number two for having the worst traffic in the United States.

For those 10,000 USPTO workers who live in homes scattered across this sprawling metropolitan area of more than 5.5 million people, working from home is a win-win for both employee and employer. Telework gives employees additional time to spend on actual work as well as family time they would otherwise spend preparing for and driving to and from the office. In addition, for an agency aggressively expanding its workforce to handle a growing backlog of patent applications, telework frees up office space for new hires who require time on campus for mentoring and training without incurring the significant costs of building expansion.

The USPTO workforce, highly professional and sought after in a competitive labor market, has many employment choices. By providing its employees a choice that does not include a two-hour commute in bumper-to-bumper traffic, USPTO can attract the talent it needs to meet its mission, accomplish its strategic goals, and hire new employees without securing additional real estate.

U.S. Patent and Trademark Organization

USPTO includes two major organizational components:

The Patent Office examines applications and grants patents on inventions when applicants are entitled to them; it also publishes, maintains, and disseminates patent information and records.

The Trademark Office reviews trademark applications for federal registration and determines whether an applicant meets the requirements for federal registration.

Additional USPTO staff offices include the Office of the Administrator for Policy and External Affairs, Office of the General Counsel, Office of Equal Employment Opportunity and Diversity, Office of the Chief Communications Officer, Office of the Chief Financial Officer, Office of the Chief Information Officer, and Office of the Chief Administrative Officer.

Fifteen Years in the Making

The "trademark work at home" (TW@H) program began more than 15 years ago when Deborah Cohn, now the Commissioner for the Trademark organization, started a pilot telework program.

In 1997, 18 Trademark examining attorneys were permitted to telework three days per week. At the time, the teleworkers accessed USPTO systems using dialup or ISDN (integrated services digital network) connections and carried their paper files to and from the office. The examining attorneys at headquarters agreed to share their single offices to support the program. This pilot program was selected as a National Performance Review Reinvention Lab during the Clinton administration and has received awards and accolades over the years since for being a model government telework program.

By 2002, when Trademark examination became more fully electronic, examining attorneys began teleworking four days a week and gave up assigned offices at headquarters; instead, they reserved shared space, a practice known as "hoteling." Most were able to connect to USPTO's intranet site, PTONet, using DSL or cable connectivity. All telework examining attorneys used government-supplied land telephone lines at home for calling applicants for trademark protection. A few Trademark service units also piloted teleworking a few days per week.

Six years later, in 2008, expanding and improving telework opportunities for all Trademark employees became a goal of the Trademark human capital strategic plan. Today, 92 percent of all Trademark staff in eligible positions telework between one and five days per week. All Trademark services work units have telework programs, and many supervisors and managers also participate in telework programs.

In 2006, Patents launched the patent hoteling program (PHP) with a goal of deploying 500 patent examiners per year to work from home full-time, improving on its previous one-day-per-week telework program. Patents has succeeded in meeting that goal each year since and now allows managers to telework as well. As of 2012, 87 percent of Patent employees in eligible positions teleworked between one and five days per week.

The Program

USPTO's success comes not so much from the program design, but from the way the organization has pursued the change to telework using a "business-unit need" approach. This approach traces its roots back to the original Trademarks pilot program and the vision of the current Commissioner for Trademarks, Deborah Cohn. It also undergirds the structure of the program. For example, USPTO's annual teleworking report addresses its numerous telework programs. Each line of business has a separate section in the report—for example, the Trademark Work at Home Program (TW@H), PHP, and the Office of the Chief Information Officer Telework Program.

Each organizational component of USPTO has shaped telework to fit its unique operating environment and constraints. This approach is also apparent in USPTO's telework policy document. Like most policy documents, it includes program scope, background, definitions, authorities, and responsibilities. But one particular statement jumps out in bold, underlined and italicized print: ***"The operational needs of the business unit are paramount."***

The expansion of telework at USPTO was also dependent on the ability of USPTO labor and management, working as a team, to create telework policy and guidelines that would ensure success for the agency and for its employees. As USPTO began to see the value of expanding telework, it realized a position was necessary to manage and coordinate the pilot programs, the data collection, and the growth of telework throughout the agency. A telework senior advisor position was created; one of the primary duties of this position was to expand telework to the corporate business units (i.e., non-Patent and non-Trademark business units such as the Office of the Chief Administrative Officer, the Office of the Chief Information Officer, the Office of External Affairs, the Office of the Under Secretary, and the Office of the Chief Communications Officer).

To ensure this expansion, the business unit heads of these offices needed to fully buy in to the program. They needed to know how telework would help them meet their business-unit goals. They needed to understand the return on investment of incorporating telework as a business strategy.

USPTO's senior telework advisor is Danette Campbell. She came to USPTO from the Metropolitan Washington Council of Governments (COG), where she helped promote the use of telework to public and private sector entities in the Washington, DC, metropolitan area. During her tenure at COG, she realized the importance of having defensible data, case studies, and return-on-investment information when presenting the business case for telework. With this information, the business unit head or agency executive can more easily make a strategic decision about incorporating telework.

While the secret to USPTO's success lies in its business-driven, strategic approach, a few common elements and themes to telework are also critical to its success. These include technology and systems specifically designed to support the teleworker; comprehensive training programs to prepare the teleworker and the manager for potential issues and challenges; active communication across USPTO on telework goals, accomplishments, and policy; and a rigorous approach to evaluating and continually improving telework programs. As Campbell points out, "telework at the USPTO is not a one-size–fits-all initiative. Just like any good program or initiative, telework at the USPTO is a work-in-progress, constantly evolving to meet the needs of our agency."

Getting the technology right is clearly an important ingredient to USPTO's telework success. Employees must be comfortable and confident that they can accomplish their work using the technology they have available to them at home. USPTO provides teleworkers with a laptop, docking station, and collaborative communication tools such as Office Communicator (a collaboration product that seamlessly integrates with email and calendars). Combined, these tools provide employees with the means to "see" when colleagues are available and communicate with them via instant messaging, email, phone, video, and desktop sharing. WebEx allows employees to attend meetings and conferences from their desktop, wherever that may be. In turn, USPTO requires the teleworker have access to high-speed cable or fiber-optic broadband internet service. Some business units provide employees with additional in-home equipment, such as printers and scanners, depending upon the business unit and the position requirements.

USPTO provides a number of supporting tools and services as well. Teleworkers can access the IT help desk between 5:30 a.m. and midnight, Monday through Friday, and 5:30 a.m. to 10:00 p.m. on weekends and all federal holidays except Thanksgiving, Christmas, and New Year's Day. USPTO has created a telework resource website that includes information technology rules of the road, user guides, and video training modules on using audio, video, desktop, and file-sharing collaboration tools. The site is a reference, education, and training tool for all USPTO employees concerning its telework and hoteling programs. The site also lists the numerous awards that USPTO has won over the years, including the Telework Exchange's prestigious Innovative Applications of Technology to Support Telework award in 2010. Teleworkers have the same access to desktop files and documents as they do when they are working on campus. For example, in the Patents line of business, teleworkers have full access to all patent information and the business systems used in the examination process.

Training and communication are central to USPTO's telework program. The typical curriculum for a new teleworker includes (1) a non-IT discussion for employees and managers and (2) IT-specific training for teleworkers. The non-IT discussion is an orientation to telework that addresses program policy and goals, employee and supervisory responsibilities, reporting requirements and techniques, data and records maintenance, security, performance management, and communication. This training is delivered live either on campus or through the Department of Commerce learning center. New teleworkers also receive comprehensive technology training, which covers hardware installation and use, VPN (virtual private network) and remote desktop connection, maintenance software, use of the computer's soft phone, WebEx, and Office Communicator collaboration tools.

Telework places higher demands on a manager's ability to motivate and monitor the workforce. Managers need to clearly define performance expectations and goals for their employees, which they then translate into documented deliverables and other results. They must build effective work teams that communicate well, are cohesive, and come together to get work done—with employees they may see only occasionally. They need to support and coach these employees through their work and their career, helping them use their time effectively, respond to work problems and challenges, and develop their professional skills. These fundamental management requirements become even more critical in a teleworking environment. USPTO helps develop and refine these skills through a non-IT facilitated discussion for managers.

USPTO has also established mechanisms to facilitate communication regarding telework. Each line of business identifies telework coordinators, who have formed a working group that meets quarterly to discuss telework issues the agency needs to address. In addition, USPTO publishes a telework annual report and shares information on telework programs and plans through a variety of communication vehicles, including business unit–specific newsletters and intranet sites. To facilitate cohesion among teleworking teams, USPTO encourages the use of collaboration tools, which enable teleworkers to maintain real-time connections with their coworkers and simulate the collegiality of an office environment.

The Results

USPTO's telework program is widely recognized as a federal human capital success story. The program has received more than a dozen formal awards from groups such as the Telework Exchange, the Alliance for Work-Life Progress, and the Telework Coalition. Numerous federal agencies have turned to USPTO for advice in starting or expanding their telework programs and have explored implementing various aspects. Members of Congress and other political leaders refer to the successes of the USPTO telework program as a leading practice. Through telework, USPTO has enhanced employee performance, achieved cost savings and avoidances by reducing office space requirements, attracted and retained a top-caliber workforce, created a distributed workforce, enhanced its organizational culture, and reduced costs and personal wear and tear associated with daily commuting. Highlights include the following:

- *Improved performance.* Historically, supervisors and managers have managed employee performance by watching what their employees do. Most managers start out uncomfortable with telework because it challenges this simple model. Although the model of watching what people do may have been common for centuries inside organizations, a very different model has been used outside organizations, in marketplaces. While the factory foreman watches everything his workers do and in that way holds them accountable, the shopper buying what the factory produces has no idea who did what or how the product being purchased was produced. The shopper focuses instead on the product itself—its quality, price, and usefulness—and makes the purchasing decision based on that assessment.

  Telework starts to move performance management towards this marketplace model, away from the more controlling and paternalistic job-foreman model. It forces managers to focus on products, results, and outcomes rather than the hour-by-hour work habits and methods of the employee. As Danette Campbell notes:

  > Our work at USPTO is very production-oriented. We have a backlog of patent applications. Some patent applications are more complex than others. But the agency understands that and has clear expectations in terms of production—quality, quantity, timeliness....I would characterize what we've done more as "rethinking the process of work." We focus on a model of clearly defined expectations and then empower employees to meet and exceed those expectations.

- *Reduced office space.* An obvious benefit of teleworking is that it reduces the cost of office space. USPTO estimates that it has been able to avoid $20 million in real estate costs as a direct result of its hoteling programs, where employees completely relinquish their office space to work from home full-time. Offices are configured with two work stations each, designed for hoteling employees to use when they are on-site. Hoteling employees schedule their time in the work space through an electronic concierge.

- *Enhanced recruitment and retention.* Initially implemented as a way to retain and attract talented examining attorneys who were spending far too much time commuting and struggling with work/life balance issues, USPTO's telework program has now grown to include all business units in the agency. Attracting and keeping talent is as important to its mission as anything else it does. According to Danette Campbell, "We have an extremely professional, highly skilled workforce. Telework is a means to help us retain the best and brightest employees. It gives us a huge competitive edge."

- *Improved emergency management.* In the winter of 2010, Washington, DC, experienced "Snowmageddon." In a single storm, more than 30 inches of snow fell on a city that panics when two or three inches blow through. The news dominated headlines for days. The *Washington Post*, in an article headlined "In Blizzard's Clouds, a Silver Lining for Teleworking," noted that "The snow may have closed Federal offices this week, but that doesn't mean Federal workers aren't working …. The Trademark Assistance Center, on the Trademark side of the Patent and Trademark Office, reported production at 85% of normal levels on Monday and Tuesday, when the government was officially closed, a spokeswoman said. That's remarkable."

A key benefit of telework that is especially important for government is emergency management. Since 9/11, agencies have been required to develop continuity-of-operations plans that document how they will respond in emergency situations to keep their operations providing essential services. If the entire workforce is in one location and can engage in its work from only that single location, emergencies can easily bring an agency's work to a halt. At USPTO, telework enabled creation of a "distributed workforce" that can continue working at full strength even if employees are unable to get to the Alexandria campus.

- *Reduced social costs.* The City of Santa Clara, California, has a website that helps commuters calculate the cost of their commutes. A major element of the overall cost of commuting is the indirect cost, borne not by the commuter directly but by governments and society at large. Those indirect costs include accidents, highway construction and maintenance, air pollution, noise, water pollution, and land use impacts. The Santa Clara website calculates the total cost of indirect costs to be 39 cents per mile. USPTO estimates that its teleworking programs reduce commuting distances traveled by its workforce by a total of 33,049,695 miles per year. Using Santa Clara's cost metric, the total indirect cost savings realized by the community as a result of the USPTO telework and hoteling programs are about $13 million per year. And that is on top of the cash that employees save directly through lower gasoline costs and reduced car maintenance.

USPTO's telework programs make major contributions to the bottom line not only for USPTO itself but also for its employees and for the community. According to Danette Campbell "Any organization whose principle tools are computers and telephones should be incorporating telework as a business strategy wherever possible."

Building a Knowledge Management Infrastructure

Social Security Administration

Paul Thompson
John Salamone

The Social Security Administration (SSA) is consistently ranked by its employees among the top 10 "Best Places to Work" in the federal government, an annual survey conducted by the Partnership for Public Service. The public likes SSA, too, ranking it near the very top among federal agencies for customer service in a 2011 survey conducted for the government IT community. If you've tried to access your earnings record on the SSA website recently and discovered how easy it has become, you will probably agree.

Successful agencies get that way and stay that way because they're always striving to get better at something, and SSA is no exception. Even in places the public never sees, deep in the organization, innovative practices take hold and change things for the better.

The Office of Labor-Management and Employee Relations (OLMER), under the deputy commissioner for human resources, is one such place. Championed by Acting Associate Commissioner Ralph Patinella and Former Associate Commissioner Milt Beever, and spearheaded by Director Jim Parikh, OLMER has launched an integrated knowledge management (KM) program to automate and streamline the way labor/management information is posted, shared, and accessed within the agency. Through this endeavor, the agency is making a concerted effort to address one of the more complex human capital–related functional areas in government: building and sustaining a KM infrastructure to improve organizational performance through collaboration and information-sharing.

The Knowledge Management Imperative

To fully grasp what OLMER has accomplished, it is important to understand some basic aspects of KM. Human organizations have been storing and retrieving information since the dawn of civilization, but KM as a recognized field of practice dates only from the early 1990s. The advent of KM coincided with the rise of the internet and the personal computer and the resulting information explosion. At the same time, "knowledge work"—a concept first described by management guru Peter Drucker in 1959—was emerging as the dominant model in the workplace. In this new world, organizations would rise or fall to the degree they could harness and use information, now available in exponentially greater quantities than ever before.

Despite its importance, KM remains a relatively little known or understood concept. Most people who work in organizations have likely heard the term, but chances are they don't have a good grasp of what it encompasses. They might define it as sitting down with subject matter experts to tap into their unique expertise and experience. That is certainly one aspect of KM, but the concept is actually much broader and more complex, encompassing everything from old standards like paper subject-matter files and standard operating procedures (SOPs) to more recent efforts to persuade subject matter experts to capture, catalog, and communicate what they know so that other individuals and the organization can benefit from their experiences.

In essence, KM is about taking what is often called "tacit" knowledge, or information possessed in isolation by one or more people in the organization, and making it "explicit"—readily available to other people through a variety of strategies and tools. Some of these strategies involve simply making information available in a file drawer, on a website, or in some other easily accessible location. Others require more active efforts to "push" information out through various communications media or "pull" or capture critical information from those individuals who possess it.

All these efforts—whatever label is attached to them—are for the purpose of capturing, organizing, processing, and readily retrieving information so the organization can use it to the fullest extent. This is the KM imperative. Not connecting the knowledge dots will inevitably lead to lost opportunities, wasted resources, and eventual decline in a resource-constrained environment.

Yet for most organizations, a systematic approach to KM remains elusive. Through the creation of the position of chief knowledge officer, a few federal agencies are starting to address KM in a more strategic and comprehensive manner. But for the most part, KM efforts like OLMER's are still in their infancy, attracting nowhere near the attention that might be gained, for example, by the latest innovation in employee performance management.

Clearly, KM depends heavily on information technology (IT). Information can now be stored in vast quantities and made instantly accessible in ways that were almost unimaginable a few decades ago. However, successful KM also depends on a thorough culture shift in most organizations—from information-hoarding to information-sharing, from isolated stovepipes to true collaboration across the agency—that may be even more difficult to achieve than putting in place effective IT tools and systems.

The OLMER Initiative

At around 65,000 employees, SSA is the largest independent (noncabinet-level) agency in the federal government and is intensely focused on its mission: providing service to its external customers. As most Americans know, these services include old age, survivor, and disability benefits as well as the need-based supplemental security income program for the aged, blind, and disabled. Less visible are the many staff offices, including the

Office of Human Resources and its components like OLMER, which provide internal products and services in support of SSA's mission.

OLMER's particular role is to manage SSA's labor-management relations/employee relations (LR/ER) program, which includes formulating policy and overseeing and evaluating program activities in the agency's 10 regions. This is a complex task, given the decentralized nature of the organization, with 1,300 field offices located virtually everywhere in the country. The Baltimore, Maryland, headquarters LR/ER staff number fewer than 40, with about 200 LR/ER specialists nationwide reporting to their respective component leadership.

When Jim Parikh joined OLMER in 2010, he found an organization that, despite its many strengths, had not yet taken the steps necessary to manage and use knowledge to the fullest. Important program information and documentation were sometimes unavailable or difficult to access. Expert knowledge and institutional memory were locked in the minds and file drawers of individual subject matter experts or savvy managers, with no systematic plan to tap into that resource and make it available to the organization at large. Work processes were in some cases still manual and lacking in efficiency and reliability. Tools and resources were needlessly duplicated in various offices across the country, resulting in much overlap as well as a failure to replicate successful local innovations across the organization.

Fortunately, Jim's training and career gave him a solid foundation for identifying these problems and setting to work on a plan to address them. During the span of his career, Jim had read extensively about KM. When he joined OLMER in 2010, he already knew of tools and techniques that would improve the flow and exchange of information among the many work units in the organization's day-to-day activities related to labor and employee relations.

Although consistency in administrative actions and adherence to precedent are paramount at OLMER, LR/ER specialists lacked ready access to information on grievances, arbitration cases, and other decisions. They also had no easy way to obtain the various labor-management agreements that were established in memoranda of understanding (MOU) around the nation. The LR/ER specialists did what they could under the circumstances, but the process was inefficient at best.

Jim also observed that OLMER was encumbered by manual processes for MOU approval/disapproval and workload tracking that failed to take advantage of the increased efficiency and consistency automation could provide. Even where efforts were made to take advantage of the "new" technology, the results were less than optimal. For example, each of the ten regions had its own website, with largely overlapping content but lacking an overarching framework.

Jim quickly realized he had to seek out someone who possessed knowledge of both IT and LR/ER work processes. The individual chosen would be tasked with automating outmoded paper-based processes and building web-based databases as well as knowledge-sharing tools that would become the platform for more effective KM. That individual turned out to be Chris Bowser. Chris' unique combination of IT skills and human resource management knowledge made him the right choice to serve as the KM IT manager for OLMER.

With Chris on board, Jim could focus on the "people" side of the effort—the organizational transformation effort whereby the various systems and solutions become mutually supportive and together form a cohesive, integrated strategy. Given the highly decentralized nature of the agency's LR/ER function, he realized that substantial effort would have to be directed to eliciting the cooperation and ultimate "buy-in" of OLMER components across the country.

Laying the Foundation for Knowledge Management

Convinced that lack of effective, consistent information-sharing was at the root of many of the problems in OLMER, in 2010

Jim launched a four-step process that would enable him and his staff to gain the understanding they needed to move forward with a KM initiative: (1) identifying key skills and organizations, (2) analyzing organizational needs, (3) making recommendations, and (4) developing strategic and tactical initiatives.

The first of these steps was probably the easiest to accomplish. Everyone in OLMER knew the roles of the various components within the organization and who the experts in the various subject matter areas were. As Jim puts it, "OLMER was known more by some of our employees as opposed to the organization. We know who the experts are and our task was to capture their expertise."

Analyzing organizational needs was a more time-intensive process, but a fruitful one. Jim and his staff conducted a series of interviews with OLMER employees, customers, and stakeholders in an effort to understand their needs and identify specific problems. They asked key questions, including: What organizational issues are holding OLMER back? What roadblocks and bottlenecks are inhibiting the free flow and utilization of information? In addition to yielding valuable insights about what to do, this exercise helped build relationships that would be vital as the initiative proceeded.

The interviews proved to be revelatory. Employees expressed a strong desire to learn something new and different, to move into other specialties. They were "hungry" to learn and to be engaged. Better KM would not be the only way to satisfy this hunger, but breaking down barriers by providing better access to valued information would certainly help.

Employees also perceived a need for more automation, to get away from inefficient paper-driven processes. It quickly became clear that it would be necessary to take the time to re-examine and possibly re-engineer the established processes.

Employees and stakeholders didn't just identify problems; they were also an excellent source of possible solutions. The recommendations compiled by OLMER staff from the interviews fell into five broad categories: storytelling, social media, knowledge repositories, knowledge fairs, and an expert exchange directory.

With the broad outlines of a plan beginning to form, it was time to reconnect and review these findings with decision makers within the organization. "We started having conversations with executives," says Jim, "to ensure we would meet their expectations." He wanted to make sure the solutions they were working on would meet the needs of both employees and management.

Implementing the Knowledge Management Program

Having received senior management support for the initiative, Jim and his staff embarked on the fourth and final phase of the developmental process: identifying strategic and tactical initiatives in each of the recommended categories to address the problems uncovered. When the final list was set, these initiatives ranged across the broad spectrum of KM initiatives—from process improvement to website development to innovative efforts to pull information from subject matter experts and push that information out to the widest possible audience of employees. Together these initiatives constitute the KM program that continues to flourish in OLMER (Figure 7-1).

While Jim himself fully embraced the concept of KM, he felt it was important to develop and communicate a message that would resonate with his staff and stakeholders. Finding that people are intimidated by the term *knowledge management*, he focused instead on getting them to embrace practical solutions to highly visible and readily understood problems—and how they and the organization would benefit from getting these problems solved. Jim's aim was to "sell KM as a product/business goal: improving collaboration in order to bring a product to market faster."

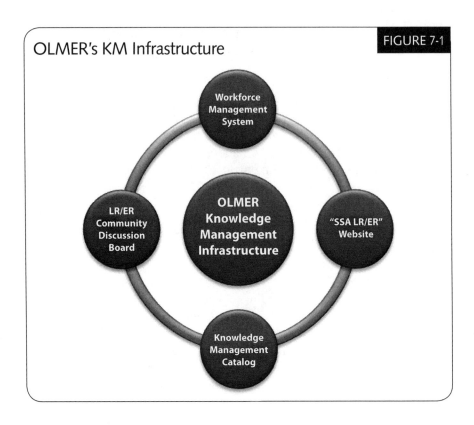

FIGURE 7-1

OLMER's KM Infrastructure

Workload Management System

The creation of the LR/ER workload management system (WMS) stands out among the OLMER KM program initiatives, not only for its positive impact on organizational work processes but also as an example of how the initiative has contributed to the transformation of OLMER's organizational culture by breaking down stovepipes. Taking advantage of a prototype system that was developed by the San Francisco region and featured at the 2010 national LR/ER conference, Jim and his staff proposed that the prototype be converted to the national LR/ER WMS.

Given the similarity of the work performed across the nation, the case for turning this homegrown innovation into a shared national system was compelling. Replacing an outmoded manual system with 14 discrete labor processes, the new system was not only demonstrably better at integrating the workflow, but has also become a vehicle for breaking down geographical stovepipes. Widely recognized as a success, the pilot system is scheduled to be implemented nationwide in 2013.

The new system offers many benefits for LR/ER managers and staff. This centralized, fully automated system captures the core business processes of the LR/ER function. It provides an automated web-based tool for staff to track and manage their assigned work. It also gives supervisors and project managers a view of progress on individual assignments and enables more even distribution of new work to staff. Additionally, it catalogs pending cases and has a sophisticated search feature.

Besides helping manage the workload on a real-time basis, the LR/ER WMS offers a vast amount of retrospective management-related information, enabling SSA to track trends and processing times as well as to analyze case decisions. The capabilities of a data-driven workload management system have overcome the initial inertia or resistance to a centralized system.

One of the many features of a work management systems like the LR/ER WMS is the ability to "embed" necessary knowledge into an automated process, much as SOPs have done over the years in organizations. Another example of embedded knowledge is the improved SOP for the MOU approval process. OLMER is responsible for approving labor-management MOUs before they go into effect. Therefore, it was only natural that OLMER should create a nationwide SOP that improves efficiency in this sensitive area. This system not only guarantees consistency in how MOUs are handled, but also interfaces at key steps along the way with the WMS to ensure that information is current.

SSA LR/ER Website

Another initiative of significant practical and symbolic importance is the SSA LR/ER website. As with the WMS, regional autonomy and sheer force of habit were barriers that had to be broken down to create this website. The challenge was to replace homegrown local IT applications with chief information officer–driven or other centralized initiatives to eliminate redundancies and universalize best practices.

Every one of the ten regions plus headquarters already had its own website for labor and employee relations. From the broader organizational perspective, this was a tremendously inefficient way to get information out; 67 percent of the content among the sites was determined to be overlapping. Having multiple sites also greatly increased the risk of providing inaccurate or outdated information.

The goal was to create a single website for one-stop shopping— an agency-level portal for disseminating up-to-date, accurate labor and employee relations information to managers, specialists, and rank-and-file employees. The goal was straightforward, but many challenges had to be addressed.

For instance, each of the regions was justifiably proud of its understanding of local employee, employment, and management issues and interests. The regions were confident that their websites accurately captured and conveyed appropriate and sufficient region-specific information. OLMER recognized this paradigm as an opportunity to leverage the information from each region by creating a central repository to share practices and procedures across the country.

Before they could gain any traction, Jim and his staff realized that they needed to balance local pride with the need for an enterprise-wide website. To ensure that the important regional elements were maintained during the web-design process, each region was represented on the One LR/ER Website workgroup, which had the task of identifying the best content for an agencywide audience. Even though the working group was large, having full regional representation allowed for more collaboration and better exchanges of ideas and information; most importantly, it fostered a spirit of ownership in the final product by all participants.

The new website, which went live in fall 2012, includes policies, procedures, training, and other resources for management and staff—more information than its many predecessors provided and at a fraction of the cost. Regions have the option to post region-specific information in addition to the agencywide content, including contact information. The site has the capability to ensure that specific LR/ER content intended as a resource for management only is offered on a restricted basis. It also has an interactive feature that allows agency program offices across the country to post information relevant to LR/ER and to share best practices.

Not content to focus solely on these signature achievements, Jim and his staff have pressed forward on several other fronts as part of their overall KM campaign. These efforts have ranged from the simple collection and storage of important data to bolder attempts to actively extract information from knowledgeable staff and push it out to the rest of the organization—or, as KM experts would say, to make tacit knowledge explicit.

To maintain momentum and continue enhancing the knowledge management repository, OLMER implemented recommendations from its customers and stakeholders. This important action served two purposes. First, it fostered additional buy-in and support from everyone. Second, it further enhanced the features of the system. For example, as a result of user recommendations, OLMER has established a virtual, searchable file of national union correspondence and another of labor-management MOUs. As a result, OLMER is now able to track and sort MOU agreements as they make their way through the approval process efficiently and effectively.

Knowledge Management Catalog

One particularly innovative repository is the KM catalog on the OLMER internal SharePoint website. This platform has been designed to enable OLMER senior experts and executives to share information on a variety of sensitive and complex labor-management and employee relations topics. Many types of information are stored in the KM catalog, such as notes and e-mails on specific ER/LR issues, tips on how to deal with particularly sensitive labor-management issues, thoughts and aspirations concerning the strategic direction of the organization, and formal program documents. For ease of use, the catalog is organized by topic and the folders are aligned with articles in the SSA labor-management contracts (e.g., leave policy, performance management).

Unlike many of the repositories, the catalog requires the active participation of the OLMER staff, specifically senior experts and executives. Getting senior-level employees to make full use of the repositories was challenging at first. However, as this initiative evolves, it is gaining momentum as potential users become more attuned to the value of sharing information as a way of promoting and learning about promising practices that might otherwise be lost.

In keeping with the recommendations, OLMER has also created a platform for "storytelling" as a way to share and disseminate information. To promote this communication strategy, OLMER establishes a platform at its national conference to showcase labor relations and employee relations challenges, opportunities, and outcomes based on specific case studies. Between the annual conferences, OLMER conducts monthly teleconferences to share information within the LR/ER community.

In addition to participating in conferences and monthly teleconferences, OLMER staff is permitted to participate in internal executive meetings as a way to obtain and transfer information. Additional vehicles include formalized training opportunities, meetings with stakeholders, and a scheduled video broadcast for training agency management and LR/ER staff (called the "LR/ER hour"). The broadcast catalog includes more than 25 in-depth and varied offerings, from collective bargaining rights and unfair labor practices to performance management to travel regulations. All these activities foster two-way sharing of knowledge and, ultimately, a culture of collaboration.

LR/ER Discussion Board

OLMER capitalizes on the power of information-sharing by hosting a labor and employee relations discussion board containing frequently asked questions on the SSA SharePoint network. The discussion board, which is currently restricted to the LR/ER community, is designed to pull in users by generating an e-mail to employees who have indicated an interest in a given topic. As with the KM catalog, getting executives and experts to take the time to weigh in is a challenge, but as the culture of knowledge-sharing continues to take hold, usage of this tool should increase.

Finally, OLMER has adopted the recommendation to create an experts exchange directory. This tool, accessible to all agency employees, describes which components perform which functions and identifies the individuals responsible for specific tasks within each component. Anyone who has spent time searching for a particular needle in the organizational haystack can readily appreciate the value of this directory, and it has already proven to be a highly popular feature of the overall KM initiative.

The Way Forward

Despite their many successes, Jim and his staff know that more work remains to ensure that the KM strategies, ideas, and practices continue to evolve and impact the mission, function, and outcomes of OLMER. In short, the office must consolidate the gains achieved and strive to increase usage of the less popular applications. "Our work will never be done," declares Jim. "We will need to continue to look at processes and continue to engage staff to see where there is room for improvement."

But clearly, a corner has been turned. The culture of information-sharing so necessary to support KM in all its facets has been planted, and Jim and his staff remain committed to continually seeking ways to reinvent themselves and their organization. As an example of their current efforts, the recently concluded national agreement with the American Federation of Government Employees became a springboard for modeling how technology can be used to deliver cost-effective knowledge transfer in a budget-constrained environment.

Using Knowledge Management Techniques

Traditionally, SSA has prided itself on maintaining a positive and constructive relationship with its employee unions; the national agreement negotiated in 2012 with the American Federation of Government Employees (AFGE) provides another example of how the agency has put knowledge management techniques to good use. OLMER created an SSA/ AFGE contract website, which includes an interactive manager's handbook that allows the user to click on contract articles that were changed from the previous agreement to find guidance and contract language interpretation.

Managers may also access videos on demand and frequently asked questions under each article to further their understanding of the new contract provisions. Originally, OLMER had planned to conduct face-to-face training on the new contract, but budget constraints forced a switch to videos instead. Not only has this approach saved money, but the videos can be reused for future managers and can as serve as refresher training for those already on board.

Key Lessons Learned

The OLMER story can serve as a source of successful "takeaways" for other agencies to study and emulate. To Jim Parikh, the foremost lesson of the KM initiative at SSA is to engage people throughout the organization and at every possible level. Roadblocks will emerge, but so too will change agents who will help provide the know-how and the energy to work around or through obstacles and sustain momentum. As Jim says, "Solutions are always there; you just have to ask the right question of the right person.

The SSA example also demonstrates the effectiveness of a multiplicity of initiatives, large and small, but all aligned to the common goal of breaking down organizational and interpersonal barriers that impede the free and beneficial flow of information across the organization. Certainly, the initiative has benefited from support at the highest levels of the agency, but it is the continual action at the local level that is helping most to transform SSA into a knowledge-sharing organization.

Another lesson is that while effective IT applications are a tremendous enabler for KM, they are not enough. It is hard to conceive of a successful contemporary KM application that doesn't make full use of IT. But as the OLMER experience conveys, IT cannot do the job alone—it must be wedded to a strong and persistent emphasis on the "people" factor.

> More challenges and opportunities lie ahead for OLMER. Jim's plans include exploring greater use of social media as a way to get managers to communicate what they know to each other. He and his staff also plan to continue expanding data portals to give managers greater access to vital information such as arbitration decisions and unfair labor practices. This is just part of a long list of planned enhancements. With continuing careful tending by the staff and the ongoing support of senior SSA management, KM will continue to flourish for the benefit of OLMER staff and agency customers.

Career Paths That Work: MyCareer@VA

8

U.S. Department of Veterans Affairs

Ben Porr
Carolyn Kurowski
Dawn Flaherty Lavelle

As with most human capital initiatives, career development is difficult to define because so many drivers influence human behavior. When looking for a new job, a person might ask himself questions like: "What jobs match my skills?" "Where do I want to live?" "What type of organization do I want to be a part of?" "How much will I get paid?" In thinking about a career, which is the compilation of a series of jobs, an individual's questions become more numerous and complex. Figuring out how and where to find answers can be daunting, especially in an organization that has over 300,000 employees operating in more than 1,400 offices across the United States.

That is the challenge the Department of Veterans Affairs (VA) faced. The second largest of the 15 cabinet departments, VA operates nationwide programs for health care, financial assistance, and burial benefits to U.S. veterans. VA has the responsibility and the honor to fulfill President Lincoln's promise, "To care for him who shall have borne the battle, and for his widow, and his orphan." With more than 1,600 distinct job titles in occupations ranging from registered nurse to cemetery caretaker to financial management specialist, VA needed to offer career development tools and resources that would meet the unique needs of diverse populations. Rather than pursue a singular career development solution, VA wanted to empower employees to take their career development into their own hands, define their own path, and make thoughtful, informed career choices. The successful end result of VA's endeavor is MyCareer@VA.

There wasn't one single "aha" moment when the idea of MyCareer@VA was conceived. The organization's long-term strategy, leadership's driving vision, and employee feedback all culminated in VA's laser focus on career development. First, VA recognized that the anticipated growth in the veteran population would mean greater demands on the department and its employees. During testimony before the House Armed Services and Veterans Affairs Committees in July 2012, Secretary Eric K. Shinseki stated, "Our history suggests that VA's requirements will continue growing for a decade or more after the operational missions in Iraq and Afghanistan are ended. Over the next five years, there is the potential for one million serving men and women to either leave military service or demobilize from active duty. The newest of our nation's Veterans are relying on VA at unprecedented levels. Most recent data indicate that, of the approximately 1.4 million Veterans who returned from deployments to Iraq and Afghanistan, roughly 67 percent are using some VA benefit or service."

VA undertook an ambitious plan to improve the service it provides to our nation's veterans by attracting, developing, and retraining its employees. Through the Transformation 21 Initiative, Secretary Shinseki challenged the department to become more people-centric, results-driven, and forward-looking. In VA's FY2010 strategic plan, Secretary Shinseki clearly identified the need for effective talent management as a top priority: "Together, VA employees will build a first-rate Department, committed to strategic human capital management including the attraction, deployment, retention, and development of our people. We will create a culture and an expectation of continual improvement in cost, productivity, response times, and first-time quality. At the heart of our organizational effort will lie the training and development of our people, so that they, in turn, can better serve Veterans. We will work to improve the management systems that enable top performance."

Another significant driver behind MyCareer@VA was the senior leaders at Veterans Affairs Learning University (VALU), who had a vision to take career development at VA to an entirely different level. Recognizing that many VA leaders are veterans themselves, they wanted to emulate the way the military provides soldiers clear guidance on what they need to do and how they need to do it effectively to move forward. The leaders' vision, at its core, was to provide current and future VA employees all that they need to explore career opportunities within the department.

The final driver that led to MyCareer@VA was employee opinion survey results indicating that VA employees were unsure of the career opportunities within VA and unclear on how to advance in the organization (Table 8-1). This feedback from employees got the attention of VA leadership, who realized that the organization needed to develop an easy-to-understand and integrated approach to career development.

Table 8-1. Federal Viewpoint Survey Data (2010)

Measures	VA Overall
Feel they are given a real opportunity to improve their skills in their organization	64%
Feel their training needs are assessed	56%
Feel their supervisors/team leaders support employee development	58%
Satisfied with opportunity to get a better job in organization	39%
Satisfied with the training they receive for their present jobs	56%

The MyCareer@VA Experience

The "why" behind the creation of a comprehensive career development system for VA is clear and compelling. So what exactly was the solution? MyCareer@VA (http://MyCareerAtVA.VA.gov) is an online resource that offers current and potential employees a one-stop shop for career planning and exploration at VA. The portal provides easy, centralized access to career development programs and resources from across the department.

MyCareer@VA is innovative because it provides users with what they need when they need it. The purpose is to provide current and potential employees enough information to get them started and a framework to guide them on their journey. Recognizing that one size does not fit all in career development, the team focused on developing a program and supporting tools that can be individualized. Also, MyCareer@VA challenged the notion that career development is solely about upward mobility. The MyCareer@VA program team decided to emphasize knowledge- and skill-building rather than simply getting that next promotion. The portal shows employees how they can build and expand their capabilities anywhere and anytime. Users find guidance on the career planning process and tools (e.g., career fit tool, career mapping tool, occupational family career guides) to help them make informed decisions about their career path.

The career planning process consists of four major steps. In the first step, individuals assess themselves (e.g., strengths, interests, qualifications) to gauge their starting point. Second, individuals examine the environment around them in terms of career opportunities at VA. Once they identify the careers that are most appealing to them, they are encouraged to develop a plan to get from where they are to where they want to be. Last, they may implement their plan through training and developmental experiences that will better equip them to take the next step in their career. Within the site, users can access the MyCareer@VA workbook to document and track progress toward their goals (Figure 8-1).

The career fit tool allows users to see what careers fit their personal preferences through a better understanding of themselves and the jobs they might enjoy at VA. After taking a short survey on their work interests and the type of job environment they prefer, users immediately see their tailored results in the form of a rank-ordered list of careers that fit their preferences. "Work

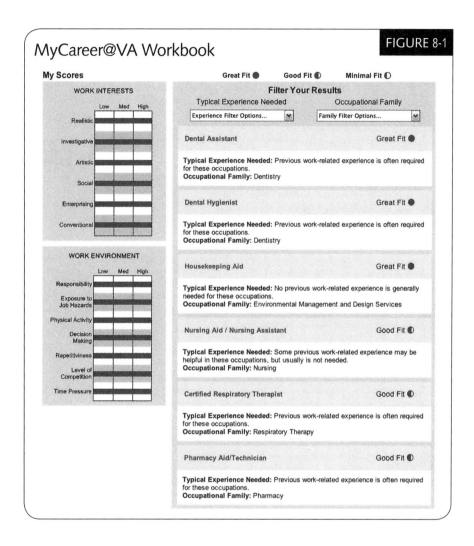

interests" refers to the types of work activities that appeal to them, such as interacting with people, thinking of new ideas, or working with their hands. "Work environment" refers to the setting in which they like to work, such as inside or outside, in a competitive or supportive environment, or in an environment with a little or a lot of time pressure.

A key capability of the portal is a robust career mapping tool, which allows users to explore career possibilities by either selecting a career path within their current occupation or exploring other occupations (Figure 8-2). The tool provides users guidance on how to progress from their current position to their desired position through recommended training and education to position themselves as a qualified candidate. A unique

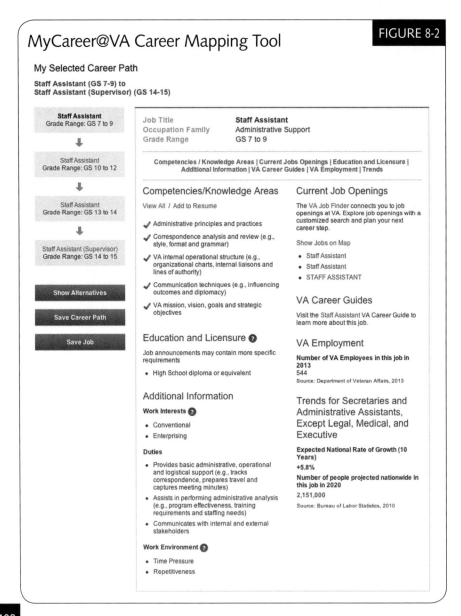

FIGURE 8-2

MyCareer@VA Career Mapping Tool

My Selected Career Path

**Staff Assistant (GS 7-9) to
Staff Assistant (Supervisor) (GS 14-15)**

Staff Assistant
Grade Range: GS 7 to 9

⬇

Staff Assistant
Grade Range: GS 10 to 12

⬇

Staff Assistant
Grade Range: GS 13 to 14

⬇

Staff Assistant (Supervisor)
Grade Range: GS 14 to 15

Show Alternatives

Save Career Path

Save Job

Job Title   **Staff Assistant**
Occupation Family   Administrative Support
Grade Range   GS 7 to 9

Competencies / Knowledge Areas | Current Jobs Openings | Education and Licensure |
Additional Information | VA Career Guides | VA Employment | Trends

Competencies/Knowledge Areas

View All / Add to Resume

✓ Administrative principles and practices

✓ Correspondence analysis and review (e.g., style, format and grammar)

✓ VA internal operational structure (e.g., organizational charts, internal liaisons and lines of authority)

✓ Communication techniques (e.g., influencing outcomes and diplomacy)

✓ VA mission, vision, goals and strategic objectives

Education and Licensure ❓

Job announcements may contain more specific requirements

- High School diploma or equivalent

Additional Information

Work Interests ❓

- Conventional
- Enterprising

Duties

- Provides basic administrative, operational and logistical support (e.g., tracks correspondence, prepares travel and captures meeting minutes)
- Assists in performing administrative analysis (e.g., program effectiveness, training requirements and staffing needs)
- Communicates with internal and external stakeholders

Work Environment ❓

- Time Pressure
- Repetitiveness

Current Job Openings

The VA Job Finder connects you to job openings at VA. Explore job openings with a customized search and plan your next career step.

Show Jobs on Map

- Staff Assistant
- Staff Assistant
- STAFF ASSISTANT

VA Career Guides

Visit the Staff Assistant VA Career Guide to learn more about this job.

VA Employment

Number of VA Employees in this job in 2013
544
Source: Department of Veteran Affairs, 2013

Trends for Secretaries and Administrative Assistants, Except Legal, Medical, and Executive

Expected National Rate of Growth (10 Years)
+5.8%
Number of people projected nationwide in this job in 2020
2,151,000
Source: Bureau of Labor Statistics, 2010

and especially helpful feature is the real-time job feed, which allows users to apply directly from the site to active job openings within VA. Since this tool is housed on the internet, potential VA employees are also able to take advantage of the resources, identifying VA jobs in which they may be interested through instant access to active vacancy announcements. They can then apply immediately via MyCareer@VA.

An additional feature of MyCareer@VA is the career guides, which provide a wealth of information, data, and statistics about each occupation. The guides include recommended developmental experiences that a current or potential employee may explore to prepare for a new career. They also provide information on position distributions across the country, recommended professional association affiliations, and specific job requirements. Users can learn how to develop their knowledge, broaden their skills, and expand their experiences to put their plan into action.

Successful Strategies

MyCareer@VA was more than a year in the making before it launched in October 2011. VALU was charged with designing, developing, and implementing the comprehensive career development portal. With buy-in from senior leadership, VALU set out to build the system in a highly inclusive and collaborative manner, leveraging the best of what already existed and building new elements to fill gaps. Despite numerous challenges, this innovative and far-reaching effort succeeded by taking several approaches:

- Getting buy-in from across the organization

- Maximizing and integrating available resources

- Never losing sight of the bigger picture for the organization.

Getting Buy-in

One of VALU's first steps was to gain leadership and stakeholder buy-in for this initiative. A challenge for VALU was that it was a new organization without a past performance track record of managing an endeavor of this magnitude. Understandably, VA's leaders asked a lot of tough questions and were cautious with their support; they wanted to be absolutely sure that the project outcome would meet the career development needs of the organization and employees. They understood the need to build a more effective workforce, but they had to be convinced that MyCareer@VA was the way to go and would be able to achieve this result. Furthermore, they wanted to be certain that VALU would be able to steward the project effectively from beginning to end.

VALU understood that MyCareer@VA would succeed only with deep and widespread support from every area in VA. Stakeholder buy-in was viewed not as a check-the-box exercise, but as an opportunity to get meaningful input to develop an optimal end product. That meant really understanding the concerns of critics and adjusting course to incorporate their feedback. In addition, expectations had to be carefully managed; the biggest MyCareer@VA fans offered valuable ideas and wanted the program to go even further.

The VALU MyCareer@VA team spent countless hours sharing the concept with stakeholders all across VA and promoting the benefits to the VA workforce. For example, well before the live portal had been developed, the MyCareer@VA team developed mock-ups of pages to show the "look and feel" and flow of the portal. Although the data hadn't been finalized and the ultimate structure hadn't been determined, the mock-ups provided stakeholders with something tangible to which they could react and provide specific input. They could literally see the tool's anticipated capabilities and how it would appear. The project progressed rapidly, and the MyCareer@VA team regularly looped back to interested parties to let them know that they had been heard and what was changed as a result.

Another successful tactic was gathering feedback from employees on the prototypes and content being collected. VALU's goal was not just to tell employees about the project, but also to provide them as full an experience as possible to mirror what it would be like to use the site. During the demonstrations, employees were invited to articulate their concerns and recommendations. The team recognized that candor was the only way to make absolutely sure that program resources would be dedicated to the highest career development priorities of VA employees rather than the "nice-to-have" features that added little value. Before the site launched, close to 100 demonstrations were conducted for a wide variety of audiences across VA. Every demonstration added to the MyCareer@VA team's knowledge of how employees would use this portal and what information would be most beneficial to them. When this feedback was shared with VALU's stakeholders, leaders were pleased to hear about how excited employees were about the future portal. The positive "buzz" had begun to spread, and with it came high expectations for what MyCareer@VA would deliver.

In addition to approaching diverse stakeholder and employee populations, it was essential for VALU to identify key influencers who saw real potential in the MyCareer@VA concept and could engage the right people in the most critical project activities. With a population of over 330,000 employees, it was neither feasible nor practical to put out a general call for volunteers. The MyCareer@VA project team needed specifically skilled individuals such as occupational subject matter experts to review and approve the job data in the tools, discerning employees to provide detailed feedback on iterations of the portal content and tools, and highly enthusiastic employees to attend launch events and participate in training. These key influencers, or "early adopters" of the MyCareer@VA concept, were essential in creating partnerships between the MyCareer@VA project team and offices and facilities across VA.

Maximizing and Integrating Resources

Before setting out to design anything for MyCareer@VA, VALU's first goal was to make sure that the team understood and accounted for the wealth of existing resources related to career development, especially in online environments, and any VA-specific tools and resources. This meant extensive data-gathering from VA contacts, reports, articles, books, databases, and websites. The team reviewed all information about online options for the development and achievement of career development goals. Even information that gave the team ideas about what not to do was useful in the idea-generation process.

VALU was well aware that many initiatives that were complete or in development at VA would support or inform MyCareer@VA. Specifically, some efforts were underway that focused on development in a specific occupation; the MyCareer@VA portal would leverage and integrate this relevant information. For example, if an occupation had already developed a competency model, the project team considered that the starting point for its efforts. In most cases, these different initiatives used different methodologies and included different information; VALU developed solutions that would account for all these unique situations. For example, when many pieces of information described a job within a career (e.g., knowledge needed, education/experience requirements, training and development opportunities), the MyCareer@VA project team created rules for how to handle this information as well as how to gather new information. This ensured standardized information across the portal while effectively leveraging all previous work.

VALU made a conscious decision early on to gather as much information as possible about VA occupations from other souces. The occupations (e.g., nursing, finance, human resources) weren't unique to VA and substantial external research had already been done. External resources such as the Department of Labor's occupational information network (O*NET), OPM's qualification standards, and ERIC's electronic dictionary of occupational titles were used to define the occupations broadly. Then, VALU used VA-specific information to begin tailoring the draft VA occupational materials. The best source of information was historical vacancy announcements. The MyCareer@VA project team compiled three years' worth of vacancy announcements, which highlighted the functions performed by job title. All these pieces of information helped the team form a broad understanding of how various occupations contributed to the overall mission of the organization.

Understanding the Bigger Picture

MyCareer@VA was one of many concurrent projects that shared Secretary Shinseki's strategic imperative for VA to become more people-centric, results-driven, and forward-looking. VALU quickly realized that building connections between MyCareer@ VA and these other important endeavors was critical. Skipping this essential step could potentially lead to redundancies, mixed messages to employees, and less than optimal use of precious resources.

It is human nature to want to be perceived as in control and confident. But when implementing a new, far-reaching program within a complex organization, it is impossible to be in control and confident at every step of the process. VALU's MyCareer@ VA team made a conscious decision at its inception to make their processes and project transparent to others. By widely and proactively communicating with other VA initiatives, VALU allowed others to poke holes in MyCareer@VA—and they did; the openness allowed the team to gather different perspectives and thereby stay one step ahead of most problems. By consistently sharing status, being up front about concerns, asking for help, and previewing future plans for the project, VALU was able to collaborate with other project teams to identify shared risks and formulate solutions before going too far down a path of no return. On occasion, a point would be raised that VALU simply hadn't taken into account. Being honest about what the MyCareer@VA team didn't know and asking for assistance from others outside the team no doubt led to a better quality final product.

MyCareer@VA is one of many IT tools that current and potential future VA employees use. Therefore, it was essential for VALU to fully understand the many internal technology systems that relate to MyCareer@VA and formulate integration strategies. For some systems, it was as straightforward as exchanging content and links to the respective sites. For others, it required understanding the complex contextual and structural nature of the systems to provide a fluid user experience. Across the board, all VA parties shared the goal of making the online experience easy and efficient to the user; many solutions were developed collaboratively. Understanding the goals and vision of the other VA IT systems enabled the VALU team to prepare for changes and future integration.

MyCareer@VA Launch

After more than a year of hard work, focus, and sometimes sheer will, the MyCareer@VA portal was ready to be launched in October 2011. Activities included a press release, a senior leadership press conference, and a series of rollout events in VA facilities around the country. These events included live presentations and interactive demonstrations by the MyCareer@VA team. The sites were chosen based on points of contact established during the development of the site who had become avid champions for the effort. This ensured that events were well attended, maximizing the impact for VA. VALU immediately began hearing from employees who were enthusiastic about the tools and the potential benefits that MyCareer@VA offered.

After the official launch, VALU implemented cost-savings outreach efforts by taking advantage of the social networks that had been developed and the virtual conferencing capability available at VA. To support the continued training of VA employees on MyCareer@VA, VALU implemented an ongoing series of live, interactive virtual training sessions. Numerous VA employees have self-selected to be "super users" and serve as ambassadors for MyCareer@VA at their facilities across the country. These super users support the program by hosting their own MyCareer@VA training events. These in-person facility-based events focus on career development within the context of that particular facility and often integrate the virtual training sessions into the event.

The Final Step: Evaluation

The final challenge was to determine if the site is meeting its goals and how to continue gathering feedback and incorporating improvements and enhancements. VALU developed and implemented a comprehensive evaluation framework to assess both the function and organizational impact of MyCareer@VA. To ensure that the portal provides the best possible career development products, evaluation efforts were conducted throughout the lifecycle of the project. Evaluation measures included:

- *User needs analyses.* During the initial stages of program design, a series of focus groups was conducted with VA employees to understand career development needs and verify the MyCareer@VA concept and functionality.

- *Content validation.* As the program and its content were developed, several feedback sessions with VA human resource experts were conducted to ensure the accuracy and usefulness of website content.

- *Usability interviews.* One-on-one usability interviews were conducted with potential users of the site to evaluate user-friendliness and initial reactions to the program and its tools.

- *User focus groups.* Upon program launch, several user focus groups were conducted with employees across VA to evaluate usage of and reactions to MyCareer@VA and all associated tools.

- *Experimental evaluation.* An experimental study was designed to gauge the personal and professional impact of MyCareer@VA. This effort compared perceptions (e.g., perceived advancement opportunities, job satisfaction) between site users and a control group. A pre- and post- assessment design was used to examine the impact attributed specifically to career development.

- *Website usage.* Website usage metrics are continuously collected and tracked as part of the evaluation effort, including number of pageviews, unique visits, and time spent on the site (Figure 8-3).

- *Website intercept survey.* A website intercept survey was conducted to assess real-time reactions from users as they navigated the website. This survey measured the effectiveness of the web portal in meeting users' career development needs.

- *Onboarding and exit process review and integration.* As part of the evaluation process, onboarding and interview processes across VA were reviewed. Recommendations were made for adding relevant career development questions to the entrance and exit surveys, allowing ongoing evaluation data for current processes to be collected.

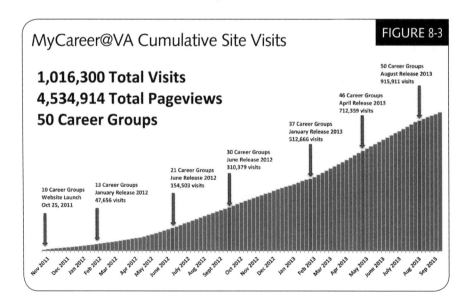

MyCareer@VA Cumulative Site Visits

FIGURE 8-3

1,016,300 Total Visits
4,534,914 Total Pageviews
50 Career Groups

50 Career Groups
August Release 2013
915,911 visits

46 Career Groups
April Release 2013
712,359 visits

37 Career Groups
January Release 2013
512,666 visits

30 Career Groups
June Release 2012
310,379 visits

21 Career Groups
June Release 2012
154,503 visits

13 Career Groups
January Release 2012
47,656 visits

10 Career Groups
Website Launch
Oct 25, 2011

- *Organizational success metrics.* To assess MyCareer@ VA's impact on overall organizational effectivess, the project team defined, collected, and tracked a range of organizational success metrics. These included employee survey data (e.g., employee viewpoint survey) and human resource metrics (e.g., turnover, promotion rates, applicant data). Continued tracking of these metrics will enable VA to determine the site's longer term impact on the organization and its strategic objectives.

Initial Results

Based on an initial ROI study conducted by the MyCareer@VA team, VALU has received the following feedback regarding the program:

- MyCareer@VA fills a critically important gap within the larger VA career development framework.

- Users external to VA are more likely to apply for VA career opportunities.

- MyCareer@VA has contributed to improved employee engagement through increased job satisfaction, improved employee-job fit, and increased comfort in taking control of personal career development.

- Increased retention could be a long-term effect of MyCareer@VA as the program increases employee awareness of advancement opportunities and perceptions of organizational support.

- MyCareer@VA plays an essential role in helping VA promote from within and maintain talented employees; costs associated with such retention have decreased.

- The site helps veterans and other external applicants overcome the complexity of the VA job structure and application process through transparency of job requirements and easily digestible resources.

MyCareer@VA was designed to provide career development options to VA employees by leveraging 21st century technology that is people-centric, results-driven, and forward-looking. This vision, articulated by Secretary Shinseki, led the MyCareer@VA team to create a first-of-its-kind collection of career management resources, programs, and training. The long-term goals and metrics that will demonstrate success of the program include the following:

- Improve engagement

  o Improving employee survey trends (e.g., advancement opportunities, job satisfaction, overall view of organization) over time with increased use of website

  o Improved attitude about the organization

- Improve retention

  o Reduced turnover

  o Increased intention to stay at VA

- Improve recruitment

  o Increasing job applications

  o Better quality of job applicants

  o Enhanced quality of internal job movement.

We may not know the full benefits of the site for many years down the road, but VA is clearly at the forefront of guiding and directing career development in new and innovative ways.

MyCareer@VA is a first-of-its-kind career development website. It was developed based on VA's strategic goals, VA leadership's vision, and employees' expressed needs. The portal has been lauded by VA senior leaders and thought leaders across government and has received numerous awards. But most important, VA employees now better understand how they can build and develop the right skills to provide the best service they can for our nation's veterans.

Job-related terminology, requirements, and processes can be very detailed and complex. MyCareer@VA demystifies career development and shows people in an easy-to-understand format what they want to see: "What are the jobs?" "How do I find the right one?" "How can I grow and develop?" The team recognizes that some people are self-motivated and learn everything from the portal, but for those who need additional guidance, the MyCareer@VA team is expanding and adding tools and resources to meet every user's needs.

An HR System That Helped Make an Agency 9

National Geospatial-Intelligence Agency

Mike McManus
Carolyn Kurowski

The National Geospatial-Intelligence Agency (NGA) plays a key role in our nation's defense and security by providing critical geospatial data both digitally and through more traditional mapping to the military services, other intelligence community agencies, and civilian agencies in time of need and emergency, such as coping with natural disasters. To meet these ever-expanding needs, NGA has gone through remarkable changes over the past 15 years. Created as the National Intelligence and Mapping Agency (NIMA) in 1996, the agency was renamed the National Geospatial-Intelligence Agency in November 2003. It was initially formed from nine different agencies or elements, each with its own systems, procedures, and culture. The new agency developed a new identity and culture, along with common systems and procedures. One key aspect of this effort was the development of a new and comprehensive human resources system that would address the needs of the new organization and help define the new agency culture.

Over the past 15 years, NGA has received notable recognition for its HR accomplishments, including the President's Quality Award, *Workforce* magazine's Optimus Award, and designation in 2009 as one of the 50 Best Places to Work by *Washingtonian* magazine. Its recently consolidated campus in the Washington, DC, area reflects the agency's success in creating an integrated, fully functioning entity. An important component of the agency's efforts over the past 15 years is a new HR management system that embodies NGA's core values, business requirements, and critical mission.

This remarkable journey required a high degree of persistence and flexibility—a willingness to apply new ideas, objectively assess their impacts, and in some cases move on and try alternatives. NGA had a clear case for change, but was faced with the challenge of developing a process for detemining the features of the new HR system and processes, deciding who would be involved in the development, and crafting a way to communicate and incorporate the resulting changes into everyday life at NGA.

Making It Real

Late in 1996, while the ink was still drying on the official documents creating NIMA, the leaders of this new agency immediately realized they had been given a once-in-a-career opportunity: Their new legal and regulatory framework gave them the flexibility to completely rethink HR. They could define their own policies for how to pay people within more flexible Title 10 limits. They could design new processes for hiring that were faster and more streamlined, and they could apply more progressive approaches to the employment contract. They could re-evaluate fundamental terms and concepts like "job," "career," "performance," and "rank." But they also realized that they faced a daunting leadership challenge: They had inherited a culturally fragmented workforce that came with many different biases, assumptions, and comfort levels regarding HR approaches and values. They were perceptive enough to see that the opportunity and the challenge were really one and that by tackling both energetically they could pull this new agency together and give it life.

The new agency's leadership first focused on coming together to reach agreement on a basic vision and philosophy for HR that could guide the agency as it worked to fill in the details.

Through a series of leadership off-site sessions, they outlined the elements they wanted to include: broad pay bands, rank-in-person, performance pay, strategic alignment, manager-owned HR processes, modern HR technology and tools, an occupational structure, and standards derived from their own requirements.

The leaders organized a large, visible effort to put some flesh on the skeleton system they had designed. They formed eight key teams, each focusing on a major HR functional area or requirement: occupational structure, performance management, pay, promotions, assignments, workforce planning, training, and hiring. The teams were staffed primarily with employees and managers from across all segments of the agency, but each team included at least one HR specialist. Union members participated on most of the teams and had input on all aspects of the process. This broad participation required additional development time and costs at the outset, but it provided many valuable perspectives that were incorporated into the design—and it proved to be critical to the eventual acceptance of the system by the workforce.

NGA conducted considerable research into alternative systems and options, and then had to determine which features were the best fit for the new agency. Which approaches best supported the goals and developing culture of the new organization? What was the most logical choice in terms of sustained administration and cost? Could the agency create a system within budget-neutral constraints that would be motivational to employees?

Several key features that NGA initially selected or that evolved to over time led to the success of the program, including:

- One band structure for all occupations

- Clear distinction between performance management and performance pay

- Performance pay algorithm that applies a midpoint principle

- Application of a bonus process that is separate from but related to salary increases

- Realistic budget

- Safety net for developing employees

- Balanced and controlled promotion process.

Developing these features typically required advanced testing, then actual application in live pay cycles and, in some cases, modification over time after results and surveys were assessed. The teams developed policy for the new agency in these areas and across the full spectrum of HR functions, from hiring policy to reduction-in-force. Their goal was to provide a new and comprehensive approach suitable for the workforce of the 21st century. Each team developed policies in their areas of expertise and all proposed policies were coordinated through the task group, NGA management, the Department of Defense (DoD), and the Office of Personnel Management (OPM).

A review of the primary features of the system, how they were developed, and how they evolved offers insights and lessons learned that can benefit other agencies working to take their HR systems to the next level.

Pay and Performance

Some pay band systems use separate band structures for different occupational groups or labor categories. While the use of multiple pay ranges is intended to apply greater precision in compensation by defining specific salary ranges by occupational groups, it can create issues with employee placement as well as administration and maintenance. When exploring options with its occupational subgroups, NGA found that this approach was controversial and divisive. To avoid the pitfalls and inherent complexity of multiple band structures, the agency decided to focus on creating a common structure for all its occupations.

By reviewing its current jobs with subject matter experts in each occupational field and focusing on where the true breaks in work occurred across all the general schedule (GS) grades, NGA was able to define all work within three very similar band structures. With a few adjustments, the three structures were consolidated into one band structure with five broad bands that reasonably reflected the pay ranges for all occupations, labor categories, and work levels. The criteria for each band could be tailored to the occupation and labor category. The processes of hiring, performance management, assignments, promotions, and career development were all applied in the context of each occupation and work level against the common band structure.

Once the structure was determined and linked to GS grades, basic administration was relatively simple; band range adjustments were made each year to reflect the changes in the GS salary structure. The band pay ranges were linked to GS grades, but were not locked into them. For example, the top salary limit in each band was raised by the equivalent of two steps over the top grade associated with that band.

NGA applied its Title 10 flexibilities to broaden the compensation range, which was supported by labor market analysis. This provided those employees who were at a top grade and step some additional salary ceiling under performance pay. The linkage of bands to grades changed over the years, with minimal complexity in the administration of the structure.

One of the key principles under the new system was to make a clear distinction between performance management and performance pay. Performance management is first and foremost a feedback mechanism to employees. While its function as an input to performance pay is important, that is not its primary purpose. NGA has always emphasized that the two processes are distinct and separate, even though there is significant linkage between them. Performance feedback is provided as soon as possible after the end of the rating period in September, and performance pay results are a separate form of feedback in January.

NGA did not fundamentally change the performance management process over the first nine years, except to refine the schedule and training and to develop a more robust review process to improve rater consistency. The ratings trend over the first five years was typical for a performance-based system. Initially about the same number of successful and excellent ratings were given, but over time most ratings shifted into the excellent score range. NGA has had to consider a fundamental question about this shift. The intent of a performance-based system is to increase performance, but how much of the increase in ratings is due to rating inflation rather than true improvements in performance? Other metrics reflected advancements in agency accomplishments overall, but it was impossible to determine how much of the advancements stemmed from changes in mission and technology and how much could be attributed to the performance-based system.

After the fifth year, ratings leveled off under the more rigorous review process, with the majority of ratings remaining in the excellent range. The conversion to the Defense Civilian Intelligence Personnel System (DCIPS) in FY2008 gave NGA an opportunity to recalibrate its ratings patterns and reinforce the concept that "successful" means the employee has successfully accomplished the assigned task or what is expected—and is not a "mediocre" rating, as some had perceived. As a result, over 40 percent of the overall ratings were in the successful range that year, and there have been only moderate increases in ratings in subsequent years, largely due to the more robust rating review process.

Alternative systems vary widely in how salary increases are determined. Some projects create a pay line that links greater total pay to higher performance or contribution. Salary increases are allocated based on this fundamental correlation within the available budget. Other systems create a more direct computation that simply applies higher salary increases for higher ratings, regardless of how high the employee's salary already is in the band. While this approach may seem logical to the employee (higher performance has a direct linear relationship to higher salary increases), it ignores the idea of a midpoint principle, where the midpoint salary range generally reflects the labor-market value of the work in the band and salary increases are moderated as employees move into higher salary levels in the band. Performance is still the primary driver for higher salary increases, but increases for any given level of performance are modified by the employee's total pay in relation to the midpoint and salary range of the band.

NGA recognized at the outset the importance of applying a midpoint principle in the salary-increase algorithm. It applies the same principle as pay-line systems, and also reflects the moderated pay progression inherent in the GS grade and step structure, where step increases within the grades are awarded at a decreasing rate over time (every year for the first three step increases, every two years for the next three step increases, and every third year for the last three step increases). It recognizes that the middle salary range of the band generally reflects labor-market rates and that the top of the band is not the target. Paying higher total salary in the band is recognition—and also an expectation—of higher performance.

Putting this theory into practice required an innovative approach. It became obvious in early pay-pool simulations that the midpoint principle could not be applied manually in a consistent way while considering all the other variables. To address this, NGA built a salary increase algorithm into a performance pay spreadsheet that allocated the available salary increase budget to employees within the pay pool based on the unique arrays of performance and position in a band for all employees, within the available budget. This provided a consistent and defensible starting point, and further adjustments could be made with documented justification for the changes.

The next major hurdle was effective communication of this principle and process to managers and employees. Their focus needed to be on the total pay of the employee, not simply the latest salary increase. Employees paid high in the band were already being paid for high levels of performance. Performance still makes a difference in the salary-increase outcome, but salary level and the available budget are also factors. The unique array of factors in any given pay pool—the budget based on the salaries of the employees, the ratings, and the salary levels in the band—all combine to create a unique array of salary decisions. These factors and characteristics of the process were continually communicated through training, websites, and reports out to the workforce at the end of each annual cycle. After General James Clapper became the Director of NGA, he took this one step further and renamed the process "total pay compensation" (TPC) to reinforce the central concept of the process.

Salary patterns established over the past 14 years at NGA bear out the validity of this approach. Unlike systems that simply focus on the salary increases and not total pay, and tend to rapidly "top out" employees at the top of the band, only about 6 percent of NGA's total workforce are topped out in the bands (with most in band 5, which does not have any further headroom with promotion within the banded structure). Attrition and new hires tend to balance out the average salary near a midpoint level in the band, and the performance pay salary computation also plays a role in that balance.

Bonuses are one-time payments that are in addition to base salary. The pay philosophy behind bonuses impacts how they are applied in different systems. Some systems treat bonuses as a form of variable pay and split a total payout to the employee between salary and bonus. The rationale for the split under this approach can be ambiguous because panels can consider performance, the salary levels within the band of the employees, and related factors as they apply the two forms of pay within specific budget limits. It is often difficult for pay pool panels to apply the funding in a logical or consistent way that can readily be explained; as a result, there is less perceived transparency in the process. In addition, many employees view the bonus portion as less valuable because it does not add on to the total salary portion that carries into future years. Another common approach is to apply bonuses only for extraordinary accomplishment or for "sustained superior performance"; they can be considered a form of annual award. This approach has a stronger link to performance and therefore a much clearer rationale.

NGA opted for this latter approach and made it the second step in the performance-pay process after the panel determined salary increases. Bonuses had a separate budget from salary increases, and the two budgets were allocated to each pay pool. In the early pay cycles, bonuses were distributed to approximately 75 percent of the population each year, which generally resulted in relatively low bonuses that were simply considered a less desirable form of payment by employees. The Director of NGA questioned the motivational value of bonuses and whether they were money well spent by the agency. He limited bonus distribution to 45 percent of the workforce in subsequent cycles, which resulted in higher, more meaningful bonuses for the workforce.

Budget is always a challenge in a federal performance pay system. Because there is no profit margin in government that can be reallocated through performance pay, some argue that performance pay is not a suitable system for government. The process has to be budget-neutral or at least budget-sensitive, which greatly limits funding options. In this context, NGA applied the funds that had been used for within-grade increases, grade-to-grade promotions that were now within the broader bands, and quality step increases to establish a salary increase budget of just under 2.4 percent of all banded employees' base pay. The bonus budget was carved out of the portion of the awards budget that was used for sustained superior performance awards. The bonus budget started out at less than 1 percent of base pay and over several years was increased to a peak of 1.9 percent in 2010; it was then reduced back to 1 percent (for bonuses and awards) with the federal pay freeze restrictions applied in 2011 and 2012.

Overall, NGA has maximized its use of available funding for salary increases and bonuses while keeping in line with other defense intelligence agencies' compensation expenditures. The fact that the average salary has remained within prescribed limits at NGA over the years validates both the salary-increase funding levels and the application of the midpoint-principle salary algorithm.

Because performance pay is awarded within a budget, it could be viewed that employees within a pay pool compete with each other to some extent for performance pay. Some critics point to this as a fundamental shortcoming, asserting that performance pay will inhibit or even destroy teamwork. Why would an employee cooperate with others if it could mean a greater share of performance pay for others? This is a dubious argument that implies that it is preferable to continue with a longevity-based system rather than risk teamwork. The reality is that several factors still encourage teamwork by individuals in a performance-pay system. Quite often the work itself requires coordinated teamwork and collaboration for the individual to succeed, which builds upon the reciprocal nature of teamwork. In addition, the success of the organization overall can enhance the ratings of the individual. For most employees, the mission is their primary goal. All these aspects of mutual benefit encourage teamwork.

NGA took steps in the design to mitigate the potentially negative impacts on teamwork. Effective teamwork has always been a part of the performance assessment, which addresses not only what you accomplish but how you accomplish tasks. Reviewers consider the impacts on overall results and the organization when approving ratings. Panels discuss the "how" as well as the "what" in pay-pool deliberations. While the perceived conflict of performance pay and teamwork will remain an ongoing academic debate, from all indications the focus on performance has not degraded teamwork in the NGA experience.

Of more concern with budget limitations is the impact on newer, developing employees, who typically cannot compete with experienced employees in the same pool for the same funds. In theory a few aspects can work to the developing employee's advantage: (1) lower performance expectations and standards at lower bands are factored into their ratings; (2) their relatively low salary position in the band salary range tends to leverage a higher salary increase in the performance-pay process when the midpoint principle is applied; and (3) eventual promotion to the full-performance band 3 represents a significant increase in salary. Nevertheless, initial pay-pool simulations indicated that developing employees generally received lower average ratings and could not keep up or catch up with more experienced employees in the same pool. Promotions to band 3 could take years to achieve, and then those employees were still relatively inexperienced at the next band work level.

Adding to this disparity was the fact that employees in comparable graded positions at other agencies had regular step increases and could rapidly advance with more promotions through several grades. Many even had regular noncompetitive career ladder advancements scheduled through a set of grades until they reached the full-performance grade.

NGA wanted to avoid a career-ladder process and culture, which typically means virtually automatic advancements on a regular schedule regardless of performance beyond a minimal level. That approach is at odds with a true performance-based system, but developing employees clearly needed some kind of safety net for advancement.

To address this dilemma, NGA developed a limited career ladder process called the occupational advancement (OA) process, which applied the salary equivalent of grade-to-grade promotions within the developmental band 2 in an annual review process. Occupations set specific expectations for advancement in terms of performance and development of proficiencies, and employees were advanced if they met the criteria. The OA employees were also eligible for performance-pay salary increases, to instill the performance culture from the outset. Once they advanced to the target-salary level in the full performance band 3, future advancement was only though performance pay and the competitive promotion process. The OA process was converted to the developmental program (DP) under the Defense Civilian Intelligence Personnel System (DCIPS) in October 2008, and the current target advancement is to the bottom of the full-performance band 3.

The OA/DP process has had mixed results. On the plus side, developing employees' pay has progressed at about 10 percent per year and they have kept pace reasonably well with graded-system salary advancement. However, over 99 percent of the

OA/DP employees are advanced each year, which brings into question whether the criteria are being applied with adequate rigor or if the process is being treated like an entitlement similar to step increases and some career-ladder advancements under a graded system. This process needs to be reviewed periodically to ensure that meaningful standards for advancement are set and followed, but in the final analysis, a safety net is required until employees have reached the full performance band; the OA/DP process achieves that intent.

Promotions

The promotion process proved to be the most controversial and challenging aspect of the new system and has consequently undergone considerable transformation at NGA. The initial intent was to establish a system similar to that used by the Central Intelligence Agency (CIA). The CIA system is considered a rank-in-person process, where employees can be assigned to higher level work and then be promoted at a later date, once they have demonstrated their performance and proficiencies at the higher work level. Promotions are considered by occupational boards in an annual process. However, in DoD that flexible-assignment approach potentially runs afoul of the merit principle of equal pay for equal work, unless the organization can moderate the job expectations to the lower grade level and add oversight. Even with those modifications, several significant issues arose with the annual promotion process for NGA.

Grade inflation was considerable over the first few years as occupations received a limit on the number of promotions, and then the selected employees were upgraded in place rather than moved to higher graded vacancies. Because occupational boards determined the promotions, the resulting structure and assignments often did not sync with operational requirements. Perhaps the most critical issue was that NGA employees felt distinctly disadvantaged when outside hires could be brought on board with a promotion, but current employees had to wait for the annual promotion process to be considered. General Clapper suspended promotions for 18 months while the agency regrouped and developed a more workable alternative. The hiatus in promotions prompted organizations to realign their positions and work more effectively; with normal attrition, some of the high band numbers fell more into line with requirements.

NGA then developed a hybrid promotion approach that included competitive promotions throughout the year and an optional annual promotion process. Organizations determined how they would promote, but both approaches required that the organization have a valid vacant position at the appropriate band level in place before they could promote. This controlled the grade-inflation issue and provided reasonable flexibility. Not surprisingly, most managers and employees preferred promotions throughout the year, so employees got promotions sooner and managers could fill positions when needed. With this change, less than 5 percent of the promotions now occur through the annual process.

Through this evolution, NGA tried the rank-in-person approach and migrated toward a more traditional DoD system that allowed visible competition for most jobs, filled them when required, and used position management to provide more effective controls on grade inflation. Employees considered the new process more transparent and thought it put them on an even playing field with outside candidates.

The more general issue is that there are fewer promotions across broad bands than under a graded structure. The broad bands provide greater salary potential with performance pay, but promotions in a graded structure provide significant salary increases along with the increased status that comes with each higher grade designation. For many employees, the higher grade status with each promotion in the graded structure is just as important as the higher pay. Some employees feel that their career paths lose some clarity with the broad band structure when they are designated a band 4 rather than specifically a GS-13 or GS-14. NGA recognizes that this is an issue for some employees, especially those who have been under a graded system, but believes the benefits and flexibilities of broad bands far outweigh those concerns. With other DCIPS organizations converting to or remaining in grades, this may continue to be an issue.

Other Changes

NGA implemented several other initiatives as part of this overall effort. The occupation structure was simplified from more than 600 position descriptions into 25 occupations that align to the new band structure. Occupational councils were created for each occupation or group of occupations to oversee occupational guidelines and functions. Occupation councils provided more specific context for the occupations within the general band structure and ensured that they aligned properly with band descriptions, performance standards, and promotion criteria. NGA revised its hiring and recruiting processes to support the new band and occupation structure and NGA's strategic workforce plan.

During this period NGA also implemented a new HR information management system, PeopleSoft. This system provided an opportunity to incorporate the newly reengineered business processes (including pay bands, performance management, performance pay, and promotions) into the new IT system.

Persistent Improvement

NGA has maintained its focus on process improvement throughout the evolution of the new processes. The promotion process provides the most dramatic example: NGA pushed forward with an entirely new approach, assessed the results, listened to feedback from all levels, and demonstrated the fortitude to suspend and radically change the approach when doing so made sense. Changes to performance management, performance pay salary increases and bonuses, and the occupational advancement process reflect more typical incremental adjustments that were implemented over time. NGA continually assessed results and solicited input from all levels of the organization.

One of the recurring inputs from employees after a few years into the process was that NGA had a good process and needed to stop implementing so many changes—employees wanted a stable process! NGA complied and pursued further changes only when there was a compelling reason. Organizations need to be careful not to be overly reactive to input, and process improvements have to be weighed against the continuity and stability of the process.

The development and implementation of the National Intelligence Civilian Compensation Program (NICCP) for the entire intelligence community and the DCIPS for the DoD intelligence community (IC) reflect the positive results of NGA's efforts. Both initiatives considered a wide variety of options for pay-band and performance-pay systems, but they eventually adopted all the key features of NGA's TPC process. The band structure, separation of performance management and performance pay, pay philosophy and salary algorithm, applying limits on bonus distribution, and including a developmental program as a safety net for new employees were all adopted in full or with minor modifications to meet the needs of the wider range of organizations. In the process, NGA incorporated a few modifications from DCIPS. The most significant change was the new performance-management system, which could be readily integrated into existing processes and allowed NGA to recalibrate its application of ratings.

The initial intent under DCIPS was to convert all DoD IC organizations to a common system, including pay bands and performance pay. Restrictions imposed by Congress did not allow that to happen completely, and while all the organizations share the same performance management process and many other policies, only NGA has maintained the pay-band structure and has performance-pay salary increases. Grades are grouped by work levels that parallel NGA's pay bands, but it could be a challenge to maintain a fully cohesive DCIPS process and interface in the future with the structural differences that currently exist.

Success Factors

NGA's long-term success can be attributed to the following key factors:

- *Management support and involvement.* Management persistence and sustained support were critical to this effort; "failure to launch" was simply not an option. NGA was fortunate to have directors who demonstrated the vision and leadership to initiate and fully support the undertaking. Top and mid-level managers were involved in the initial formulation of the NIMA organization, and they set out the framework for further development.

- *Involvement at all levels.* An HR team spearheaded the development and implementation effort, but this was by no means simply an HR action or process. More than 100 employees and managers worked on one of eight teams for over a year to develop the key aspects of the new systems, including occupation structure, performance management, performance pay, and related functions such as communications. The participants gained ownership and became champions for the new system. Union members participated fully.

- *Continual but smart communication.* NGA found that effective communication requires not only continual updates, but good judgment on how much to communicate. Some employees felt inundated with information and started ignoring the updates. The communications team quickly realized that "firehosing" information to the workforce was not as effective as providing focused, concise communication on key areas of interest, with links to more detailed information for those who needed it. Posted questions and answers proved to be another effective method of communication.

- *Concise, relevant, and timely training.* NGA developed a suite of training options for employees and managers on the key features of the processes. Performance-management training outlined the steps in the process and the roles that both employees and managers played in the process, from collaborative planning sessions at the outset to employee self-reporting of accomplishments at the end of the rating period. Pay-pool panels received training on performance-pay principles and procedures as well as on use of the performance-pay spreadsheet. Optional pay-spreadsheet demonstrations sessions are also available to employees. A mix of computer-based training and actual classroom training is available on most topics. One of the keys to effective training is timing: Classes are provided just before required actions in the cycle, which makes the training much more relevant and effective.

- *Application of required resources.* Significant resources were required to develop and implement the new systems, but NGA recognized that they could not shortchange the process and hope for success. The following were the chief cost areas:

  o The time and effort that management devoted to this initiative was a significant and invaluable resource, but that was only the start of the labor requirements. NGA devoted a significant number of employees and resources to the teams in the developmental phase. This resulted in initiatives that were fully vetted and created a general sense of ownership among the workforce.

  o Performance management can impact almost every other process, and NGA soon realized that adequate resources and time had to be provided to administer the process. This includes the time supervisors need to devote to the planning, continual feedback, and final evaluations in the process, as well as the effort that employees need to put into the process, from participation in the planning stage through the input of their employee accomplishments.

  o NGA had to maintain a delicate balance between providing meaningful incentives through pay and remaining essentially budget-neutral. Conventional wisdom at the time indicated that salary budgets had to be at least 2.5 percent of total base pay to motivate the workforce, and some references claimed that 5 percent or more in funding was required. NGA found that it could pay almost 2.4 percent in salary increases each year and remain budget-neutral. From all indications, this level provided sufficient critical mass to motivate NGA employees under performance pay. A separate bonus budget applied through the same annual process helped reinforce pay-for-performance principles. That budget was primarily funded from awards funding.

o   IT support requirements are typically underestimated at the outset in terms of both cost and time required to implement. NGA had a skilled and dedicated staff and contractor support who met seemingly impossible requirements and deadlines. One key reason for success in this area is that IT specialists participated as members of the design team from the outset, and IT concerns and limitations were factored into the initial design and implementation schedule.

• *Willingness to take reasonable risks and make adjustments.* While the key principles initially implemented in the NGA processes remain intact, some aspects have been tried, assessed, and changed. This has actually proven to be a strength of the process, because it allowed NGA to experiment with a variety of approaches and ultimately develop a more effective system. It proved to be selection of the fittest applied in the government sector. One example is the evolution of the NGA promotion process. NGA took the initiative to implement an entirely new process, and then took an even bolder move to stand down on the promotion process for over a year to regroup and make necessary changes.

- *Safeguards in the processes.* Several safeguards were incorporated into the processes to protect individuals and enforce consistency. The performance-management process has at least three levels of assessment and review: the rater, a reviewer, and a performance management performance review authority (PM PRA) to review ratings across a broader group to ensure that standards are applied consistently and the narratives justify the ratings. Pay decisions are made by panels rather than individual managers, and those decisions are subject to higher level reviews by performance pay performance review authorities (PP PRAs). The pay pools are established at the lowest level practical to help ensure that the panel members are familiar with the employees' work accomplishments. Grievance and appeal procedures are established and clearly communicated, and they are administered on a timely basis within well-defined timeframes.

- *Continual process improvement.* NGA regularly reviews all of its processes to determine if any improvements are required. Performance management, performance pay,

Key Achievements of the NGA Initiative

- Created a common agency identity and reinforced a performance-based culture

- Involved the workforce in the development and refinement of the processes

- Established one comprehensive band structure for all occupations

- Incorporated agency strategic goals into performance management and performance pay

- Developed a pay algorithm that rewards performance and applies a midpoint principle

- Completed 14 cycles of performance pay deliberations by the end of 2012

- Implemented effective review processes for performance management and performance pay

- Provided appropriate advancement for developing employees

- Continually conducted process assessment and process improvement

- Provided a framework for the Defense Civilian Intelligence Personnel System

and promotion results are assessed each year and input is obtained from managers, boards, panels, HR personnel, and employees through questionnaires, focus sessions, and the website. NGA has found that balance and deliberation are necessary in making changes, and that change has to be weighed against stability

Results and Key Lessons

Pay bands were initially implemented at NGA in November 1998, and the agency entered its 14th pay cycle in fiscal year 2012. At this point, well over half of NGA's employees have never been under a graded structure at NGA, and pay bands and performance pay are an established way of life. Even though the performance culture is mature, NGA continues to assess the effectiveness of pay bands and performance pay in relation to continual changes to missions, budgets, workforce, labor markets, and related processes. Effective performance management continues to be the key area of focus for process improvements.

The NGA experience highlights some important lessons learned that may be applicable to other organizations:

- Making a compelling case for change can be half the battle. NGA was fortunate to have a clear and imminent need that had to be addressed.

- Full engagement by all levels at the outset helps establish a sense of ownership by all, which is critical to the ultimate success of the system.

- There is no perfect system. Even good systems need to be reviewed for logical process improvements, but reasonable stability is also an important factor.

- Change will result in some missteps. No one can expect to get it right 100 percent of the time. The more critical issue is how organizations respond to challenges and if they are able to leverage those challenges into opportunities to improve.

Many believe that the federal personnel system that was initiated in 1949 for a largely clerical workforce is not a good fit for today's professional federal workforce and more advanced agency roles and strategic goals. Other agencies and even the federal government as a whole may conclude at some point that their human resource systems are not meeting current and future needs and that they need to forge ahead with a new approach and a new system. The principles, methodology, and processes developed by NGA provide a blueprint for success that can be applied to such initiatives.

Contribution-Based Compensation

Air Force Research Laboratory

Tim Barnhart
Mike McManus

When talking about pay and performance, the late Dr. George Abrahamson liked to characterize managers and employees as performance co-conspirators. Dr. Abrahamson had been around the block a few times: Director of the Poulter Laboratory and Senior Vice President of the Sciences Group at Stanford Research Institute (SRI), chief scientist for the U.S. Air Force, and a return at the end of his career to SRI as senior technical advisor. But people at the Air Force Research Laboratory (AFRL) remember George best for inspiring AFRL's contribution-based compensation (CCS) system.

Performance is traditionally defined as a measure of how well an employee accomplishes a set of tasks. An employee who performs assigned tasks well is considered a good performer; an employee who performs assigned tasks poorly is considered a poor performer. Managers strive to get the most work they possibly can out of their group of employees. A good manager plays on employees' strengths by designing jobs that allow each employee to succeed. If a football player is best at blocking, you make him an offensive lineman; if he is good at dodging and juking, you make him a running back. But as George so often pointed out, the result is that employees always end up in jobs they can perform well. Hence managers and employees are co-conspirators—conspiring so that performance, defined in this traditional way, is always good.

The problem arises when pay is tied to this traditional measure of performance. If everyone succeeds in performing assigned job tasks, how does the measure of that performance provide any insight into how much an employee should be paid? Once the conspiracy concept is understood, as George so often pointed out, it becomes clear that the proper basis for determining pay is not traditional performance—how well an employee does what he or she is told to do—but contribution—how that employee contributes to the organization and its mission.

In the 15 years that AFRL has been using CCS, the federal government has tried, unsuccessfully, to implement pay-for-performance systems at the Department of Defense (DoD) and the Department of Homeland Security. Even in the business world, doubts have emerged regarding pay-for-performance, as studies have shown that it demotivates employees and interferes with meaningful feedback on performance and development. Given the current sentiment on pay-for-performance, AFRL's accomplishments stand out even more prominently. For 15 years, AFRL has been carefully measuring the contributions of its employees and paying them more when they contribute more. For these same 15 years, leaders, managers, and employees have all reported extremely positive results and high levels of satisfaction with the critical elements of CCS.

How Does CCS Work?

The Defense Authorization Act of 1995 authorized DoD to establish personnel demonstration projects in research laboratories. This permitted those laboratories to experiment with HR management practices and policies that would not otherwise have been allowed under the statutes governing personnel management in the federal government (Title 5 U.S.C.). Using this demonstration project authority, AFRL designed its CCS and implemented it in March 1997.

AFRL's CCS design reflects the contribution-based approach George Abrahamson first applied during his tenure at SRI. The fundamental design of the system is relatively simple, although the specific tools and processes used can seem complex.

Every year, individual employees are evaluated, much like they would be under a traditional performance appraisal system, except that the standards used for the evaluation are designed to measure the employee's contribution to the mission and goals of AFRL rather than success in performing the specific objectives of a given job. As a result of this evaluation, each employee receives a contribution score that places his or her contribution along a broad continuum representing the full range of possible contribution levels at AFRL. The employee's contribution level is then compared with his/her compensation level. If the employee's contribution level exceeds his compensation level, his pay is increased so that his new pay properly reflects his current contribution level. If the employee's contribution level is below his compensation level, then he receives no pay increase until his contribution catches up to his pay. That's the basic design, as depicted in AFRL's operational manual (Figure 10-1).

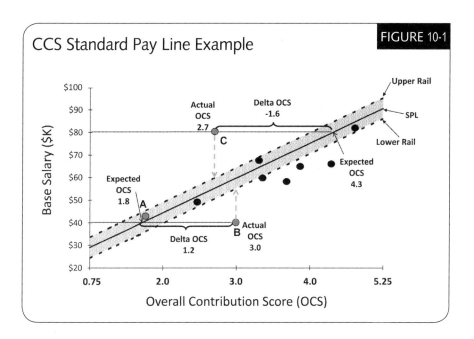

CCS Standard Pay Line Example

FIGURE 10-1

The y-axis represents the range of possible pay levels for the work covered by AFRL's system. In this case, the range includes all possible pay levels for scientists and engineers; it spans the pay range for GS-7 to the pay range for GS-15. The x-axis represents the range of possible contribution scores AFRL's scientists and engineers can receive, and it spans a score of 1 to a score of 5. The diagonal line in the middle of the chart, running upward from left to right, is known as the standard pay line (SPL). That line establishes the normal expected relationship between an employee's contribution score and his or her compensation. For example, an employee with a contribution score of 3 should be paid $60,000, which can be determined by following the vertical line upward from the 3 score on the x-axis to the point where it intersects the SPL, then moving to the left to locate the compensation level on the y-coordinate corresponding to that point on the SPL. In this way, the expected compensation level for all employees in the system can be determined based on their contribution scores.

The two diagonal lines running in parallel to the SPL are known as the upper rail and the lower rail, and the space between them is known as the equitably compensated area. The purpose of these lines is to soften the implied precision of the SPL. What the upper and lower rails communicate, using the same example, is that an employee with a contribution score of 3 would be equitably compensated if paid anywhere between approximately $55,000 (the lower rail) and $65,000 (the upper rail), rather than suggesting that the employee must be paid exactly $60,000 (the SPL).

The chart also includes three dots, labeled "A," "B," and "C." These dots represent three hypothetical employees who have been plotted on the chart to reflect their current compensation levels and their contribution scores. Employee A, for example, is paid approximately $40,000 and has received a contribution score of approximately 1.8. This places Employee A in the equitably compensated area, suggesting that Employee A's pay is consistent with her level of contribution. Employee B, however, falls below the lower rail into an area known as the under-compensated area. This suggests that Employee B is not paid enough for what she is contributing and should be paid more. Employee C falls above the upper rail into an area known as the overcompensated area. This suggests that Employee C is paid too much for what she is contributing and should either step up her contribution or be paid less. The dashed lines point to the target pay range on the pay line based on contribution.

By plotting individual employees according to their contribution scores and compensation levels, AFRL managers can clearly identify where they need to focus their available compensation dollars to bring pay into alignment with contribution. AFRL has established policy on exactly how to make compensation decisions within this framework. The basic principle is that those in the equitably compensated range receive the general pay increase granted to all federal employees, and the funds that would have gone into step increases and promotions are now pooled and used to move those who fall in the undercompensated area into the equitably compensated area. Those who fall in the overcompensated area receive no pay increase. This is an oversimplification of the exact mechanics of CCS, but it reflects the general principles that guide AFRL's policy.

Using CCS, AFRL plots the entire workforce according to their contribution and compensation (Figure 10-2). The outliers become clearly identifiable, helping AFRL understand where to focus its compensation resources and highlighting performance issues it needs to address.

Employees are constantly moving through the middle area between the rails. Those employees below the lower rail are most likely employees who have stepped up their contribution, moving their score to the right, and the chart indicates that their compensation needs to move up to reflect this increased contribution. For those above the upper rail, the message is usually received loud and clear that they either need to increase their contribution to justify their pay or they need to move to another position. Attrition rates for those in the overcompensated area run as high as 50 percent per year. While the overall pattern may remain similar from year to year, high performers are constantly moving up and low performers are constantly moving

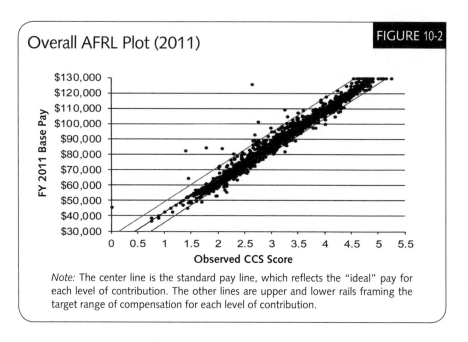

Overall AFRL Plot (2011)

FIGURE 10-2

Note: The center line is the standard pay line, which reflects the "ideal" pay for each level of contribution. The other lines are upper and lower rails framing the target range of compensation for each level of contribution.

out, which is exactly what keeps those dots clustered in the equitably compensated area.

Measuring Contribution

The hard part of CCS is how to measure contribution. First, this measurement is very different from the traditional concept of performance. Traditional performance measures quality, quantity, and timeliness. Traditional performance may also measure success in achieving agreed-upon results, such as producing a report or making a sale. What traditional performance almost never measures is the value of the employee's work to the organization. Two different people may fully meet their performance goals; traditional performance doesn't seem to care whether those two successes are of equal or wildly different value to the organization.

The concept of contribution is to begin where performance ends. While performance focuses on measuring how well you did what you did and assumes that its value is accounted for elsewhere, contribution ensures that you did your work well and then focuses on measuring the value of those work accomplishments. It's all about impact of an employee's work on the organization's mission and goals.

Contribution tends to measure the same kinds of things that a traditional HR system measures through job evaluation systems for purposes of employee progression through defined career levels. For example, the traditional federal position classification system measures the level of knowledge a job requires, the degree of supervision required, and the scope and impact of the work. These sorts of factors are naturally aligned with the degree of impact the work has on the agency's mission results. A job that requires a high level of knowledge, operates independently of direct supervision, and has broad scope is likely to have a greater impact on the agency's mission.

The following specific factors that AFRL uses to measure employee contribution align closely with traditional job evaluation factors:

- *Factor 1: Problem solving.* Measures project scope and level of impact, technical complexity and creativity, and recognition of work.

- *Factor 2: Communications.* Measures contributions to scientific papers and reports, breadth of responsibility, level and diversity of audiences for scientific work, and level of oversight required.

- *Factor 3: Technology management.* Measures contract and technology management responsibilities.

- *Factor 4: Teamwork and leadership.* Measures role on project teams, breadth of influence, supervision exercised, and guidance received.

These factors are not measured along a qualitative scale with markers such as "acceptable" or "outstanding," but rather along a value scale with four defined levels. The value scale spans the full range of contribution that might be expected for the broad career field of science and engineering as applied at the lab, including the contributions usually associated with new entry-level employees as well the contributions of experienced scientists and scientific leaders. By contrast, traditional performance management systems define a performance range that might be expected for a single job title at a particular grade level. Unlike a narrow performance scale, the contribution scale is a tool for total management of an employee's career development and progression as well as for determining annual pay adjustments and bonuses.

At AFRL, this contribution scale is applied by teams of managers evaluating groups of employees within a major organizational unit. This approach ensures a high degree of consistency in how the contribution factors are applied. The contribution assessment begins with a self-assessment by the employee, with inputs from the employee's team leader to ensure that all contributions have been captured and well articulated. The employee's immediate supervisor then assesses the employee's contribution against the contribution factors in the AFRL scale and assigns a preliminary contribution level for each factor. Following the immediate supervisor's assessment, the branch head and all the section heads within the branch meet to review and calibrate the contribution levels of all employees in the branch. This group review by managers is repeated again at the division level, with the division head and all the branch heads participating.

Through this collaborative process, a contribution score is developed for each employee in each factor, along a scale of 1–5 and with up to one decimal place. For example, an employee might receive a score of 3.2 on one factor, 3.9 on another, and 2.4 on another. All the scores are averaged to determine the employee's final contribution score.

Another value-added feature of the contribution-based approach is that it allows the organization to rank-order its entire workforce. All employees in a division, for example, can be listed in rank order by their contribution score as a way of intuitively validating the results of the contribution assessment and reaching agreement that the relative contributions of different employees have been accurately recognized in their respective scores.

Once the contribution score has been determined, the pay-pool manager (a senior military leader or senior executive designated to manage the CCS process for the pay pool) convenes a meeting with the division heads to review each employee's compensation and contribution in relation to the standard pay line. Pay adjustments are determined, with the goal of moving all employees closer to the standard pay line.

AFRL Results

Since implementing the CCS system in 1997, AFRL has conducted detailed annual evaluations to assess its impact and effectiveness and to determine its potential value for other parts of the government. Fourteen annual evaluation reports have now been prepared.

The highlights of the impact the CCS system has had over the years include the following:

- Employee grievances gradually dropped by approximately 50 percent and formal complaints (equal employment opportunities and unfair labor practices) disappeared entirely for a seven-year stretch, briefly reappearing when CCS was expanded to include nonscientific and nonengineering employees.

- Comparisons of AFRL to control-group populations consistently show significantly higher levels of management satisfaction with the CCS approach (50 percent higher or more), particularly in areas such as authority to set pay and authority to advance employees.

- Despite added management flexibilities, salaries at AFRL have remained in line with the salaries for government scientists and engineers at comparable organizations such as NASA and the Department of Energy.

- Mean contribution scores at AFRL have risen over the life of the system. The dispersion of contribution scores has also increased, suggesting that the contribution factors have become more effective over time in differentiating among employees, even as mean scores increased.

Michelle Williams has been Director of the AFRL demonstration project office since 2004. She comments:

CCS is such a central part of the lab now, that I can't imagine what life here would be like if we had to go back to the old GS system. Everybody—both managers and employees—is so comfortable with this concept and the processes we use. It feels natural and intuitive to people. Many people here don't know any approach except for CCS.

Once we got through the initial transitions back in the late '90s, we quickly reached an acceptance rate of almost 80 percent, meaning 80 percent of our employees felt positive about the system overall. Employees like it because it gives them meaningful feedback about their career progression. In school you might have received an A or B or C in a particular class, but what you would've really valued is some feedback on whether you were ready for college, what you needed to do to succeed in college, whether you should look ahead to graduate school, or perhaps whether you could move through college in three years instead of four. You needed feedback that could help you plan for your continued growth. That's what CCS encourages. Managers and employees have conversations about that sort of thing, not just about employees' short-term performance.

Managers like it because they have complete pay-setting authority. They can offer much more competitive starting salaries than they could under the old system, and they can promote their star employees faster. We've also found that this system allows much more flexibility for dual tracking. Many of our scientists and engineers can contribute just as much in nonmanagement roles as they can in management roles. It's very common to have teams where the manager is second, third, or fourth highest paid employee on the team. People gravitate to roles that match their interests and strengths, but they still find ways to make major contributions in those different roles.

Advantages and Limitations of CCS

For most of us, if we think back on our careers, we will recognize that the progress we have made was driven primarily by our professional growth and maturity, not by the particulars we accomplished one year versus the other. Over time we increased our professional value because we demonstrated we could take on larger roles and contribute more to our organization. This professional growth was probably recognized by a series of promotions; any significant jumps we may have experienced in our compensation were the direct result of those promotions.

Contribution-based compensation is a systematic way of assessing, managing, and recognizing this long-term pattern of professional growth. That is the system's true strength. In the past, similar approaches were called "rank-in-person" systems. Their focus was on recognizing the increased value individual employees demonstrated and letting that increased value drive the employee's rank, rather than having rank be driven exclusively by the job an employee was assigned. CCS does exactly the same thing but within a defined framework that enables managers to determine and communicate contribution in a consistent and systematic way. It's a rank-in-person system that can be easily understood and consistently administered. Exhibit 10-A offers a quick comparison of CCS with traditional pay-for-performance approaches.

If CCS is rightfully placed in the context of career progression, it quickly becomes immune from many of the criticisms traditionally leveled against pay-for-performance. After all, the critics of pay-for-performance are not critical of career progression and the importance of paying more for work of a higher level or value. Their criticism is focused on the more narrow practice of trying to pay more or less for the same level of work, through a measure of how well that work was done.

Daniel Pink's recent book, *Drive: The Surprising Truth About What Motivates Us* (Riverhead Books, 2009), offers one of the better arguments against pay-for-performance. Pink contends that extrinsic incentives are not nearly as effective as intrinsic incentives. Extrinsic incentives, he says, can be counterproductive. Some of the scientific literature he cites likens the phenomenon to stage fright. People who can sing beautifully in the privacy of their home may choke when put before an audience. Likewise, employees may find that powerful financial incentives cause them to choke on the job and perform less effectively than they would in the absence of such incentives.

Pink argues that organizations would be much more effective if they focused on inspiring their employees by nurturing intrinsic incentives, rather than controlling them through intricate "carrots and sticks" performance systems that reward or punish specific actions or behaviors. He goes on to explain what kinds of intrinsic incentives are most effective, breaking them down into the following:

- *Autonomy*, the satisfaction of having some control over what one does and how one works

- *Mastery*, the satisfaction of getting better and better at doing something

- *Purpose*, the satisfaction of doing something that matters.

The way in which CCS differs from traditional pay-for-performance systems aligns with Pink's notion of intrinsic incentives. Compare CCS to the three elements of intrinsic motivation that Pink identifies:

- *Autonomy*. A critical element of CCS is that employees have a high degree of freedom to shape their career growth and development. They are not placed in narrowly defined jobs with narrow performance standards. The general direction they are given is to further the research goals of the laboratory. CCS contribution factors simply provide a framework to help them understand how to contribute, over the course of their entire career, to the specific goals that are important to the lab. But employees remain free to define many of the details of their career path.

- *Mastery*. In CCS, increased contribution equals increased mastery. The contribution factors serve as a framework for defining and measuring mastery in the context of AFRL. Employees are driven by the intrinsic motivation of achieving mastery; CCS simply recognizes, after the fact, when that mastery has occurred.

- *Purpose*. Higher contribution also equals higher purpose. The progressive contribution levels within AFRL's CCS serve as descriptors of higher and higher purpose—higher and higher impact not only on AFRL's goals but on DoD's goals and on the safety and security of our country. For those who are motivated by having an impact, CCS empowers them to find ways to have that impact, recognizes when they have done so, and pays them more for it.

Neither Pink nor any of the other critics of pay-for-performance are critics of paying some people more and other people less. They acknowledge, for example, that market factors are a legitimate basis for determining pay. They also agree that career and professional growth are legitimate differentiators of pay. The brand-new employee fresh out of school should be paid less than the experienced veteran who has demonstrated what he or she can do. This is exactly what CCS does. Another way to understand CCS is as a well-defined internal labor marketplace. It provides definition of the kind of work that is more or less valuable in the AFRL marketplace and empowers employees to work within that market to pursue their own goals and interests— knowing how the market will reward them for the things they choose.

CCS has worked exceptionally well at AFRL and is clearly well-suited to the laboratory environment. Many other DoD laboratories have adopted CCS or versions of it, including the Naval Research Laboratory, the U.S. Army Tank Automotive Research Development and Engineering Center, and the Naval Sea Systems Command. In addition, the acquisition workforce in selected organizations throughout DoD is compensated under an approach similar to CCS.

However, CCS is not for every organization. The system would likely not work so well in a highly structured production environment. It is well suited to knowledge workers and to organizations that perform creative, design, or strategic functions. Any dynamic business environment that requires employees to continually develop, grow, take on new tasks, adapt to change, and respond to new customer requirements is an excellent candidate for a contribution-based model. Contribution-based models pull employees out of their position boxes and place them in much larger mission and business boxes. The message is not: Do what is in your position description, do it well, and we will reward you. Instead, the message is: Take initiative to bring about results that impact the mission and we will pay you what that is worth.

AFRL's contribution-based compensation system was once an experiment, but it long ago matured into a leading practice. Surprisingly, it is a somewhat invisible leading practice outside the DoD research and development community. Much of the rest of government could learn valuable lessons from the successes that have been achieved at AFRL. With the demise of DoD's National Security Personnel System, most of the federal government is left with a pay system designed in 1942, whose conceptual underpinnings are woefully out of date. CCS, by contrast, represents a concept for performance and compensation that is on the cutting edge, not just in government but also across industry. Current trends in the economy, the importance of knowledge workers, and the increasingly important roles of creativity and innovation in organizational success all come together to make the case that more and more government agencies and private businesses should give the CCS methodology a careful look.

The CCS system also includes some process techniques that have proven very effective and could be replicated in traditional performance appraisal systems even for organizations that are not ready to adopt the full CCS concept in its entirety. Chief among these is the way CCS relies on groups of managers to develop the CCS rating, rather than expecting an employee's immediate supervisor to develop the rating in isolation. This solves the problem of easy-versus-hard raters by calibrating rater understanding of the contribution standards and by inviting multiple perspectives and inputs, similar to 360 degree assessment systems. Also, CCS openly encourages managers to compare employees with one another using techniques such as rank ordering of employees to help raters further validate their contribution ratings.

Exhibit 10-A
Key Features of CCS versus Traditional Pay-for-Performance

Performance	Contribution
Defined relative to the job	*Defined relative to the mission*

In pay-for-performance systems, the performance appraisal is always conducted in the context of the job. It asks, "Did you do your job well?" Contribution-based pay systems look beyond the job. The question becomes, "What is the value of what you did in terms of accomplishing the mission?" If you transformed your job into one of higher value, it recognizes that. If you diminished your job into one of lesser value, it recognizes that. If you took on an entirely new job, it recognizes that as well.

Performance	Contribution
Measures quality, quantity, and timeliness	*Measures level of work and value of results*

Most performance appraisal measures focus on quality, quantity, and timeliness: "Did you do a good job?" "Were you productive?" "Were you timely?" Contribution assessments look at the level of work done and its value. In this sense, contribution assessment is similar to the old position classification evaluations designed to determine the appropriate level of a position. In fact, many of the contribution factors used in the DoD laboratories look strikingly similar to factors in position classification standards.

Performance	Contribution
Presumes a system of position classification	*Replaces a system of position classification*

Since performance appraisal systems do not look at the level or value of work, they presume that the level-of-work dimension has been accounted for through a position classification. Position classification determines that a given job is at a certain level and is thus worth a certain range of pay. Performance appraisal then only needs to focus on helping determine where in that range the employee's pay should fall, assuming higher performers are worth more in that range than lower performers.

Since contribution-based pay systems look explicitly at the level or value of work, they do not presume a position classification system that determines grade level. In fact, they replace position classification. Under contribution-based systems, there is no need for traditional position classification because an employee's contribution score determines what band level his or her position is at, not vice versa. For this reason, contribution-based systems are ideally suited for broad pay-banding constructs. In broad pay-banding, important distinctions among different levels of work often get lost because pay ranges are so broad. Contribution-based systems provide a methodology for reintroducing level-of-work considerations into pay-setting.

Performance	Contribution
Different factors and standards for different jobs at different levels	*One unified set of factors and standards across many jobs and levels*

Because performance is defined relative to the job, the factors and standards used to measure performance must also be job-specific. For example, an office assistant may have a performance factor that measures typing errors while a management analyst may have a performance factor that measures the depth and thoroughness of studies conducted. Because each is being measured in the context of the job being performed, it would be impossible to develop a common set of performance factors that apply to both the office assistant and the management analyst.

Under contribution-based systems, the opposite is true. A single set of factors and standards must be applicable to very broad sets of jobs in order to compare the value of work done and place it along a complete continuum. Both the office assistant and the management analyst would be measured against the same factors (e.g., leadership) to determine their relative value to the organization.

Performance	Contribution
Impacts pay within the pay range set for the job	*Impacts pay and promotion across the entire pay range*

Again, because performance appraisal does not measure the value of work, it cannot be used as a definitive indicator of pay. Rather, it indicates only if someone should be paid higher or lower in the pay range. Contribution assessments, on the other hand, impact pay across the organization's entire pay range. An employee's contribution score answers the question, "How much should this employee be paid?" If the employee's pay is higher than the pay range for the position, the employee should get promoted. The contribution score drives pay within the range for a band, as well as movement to the next band.

Performance	Contribution
Pays again and again for the same performance	*Pays only for increases in contribution*

Under performance-based pay systems, employees who perform at the same level year after year will get the same performance rating year after year and thus the same accompanying pay increases. Under contribution-based pay systems, pay increases are the result of the delta between contribution and pay. So the employee whose contributions are at a given level year after year will continue to be paid at that level until the level of contribution increases.

Performance	Contribution
Pay is a symbolic reward—recognition for a job well done	*Pay is just compensation—an assessment of how much should be paid given the value of the employee*

Because performance pay involves adjustments only within a range, it is best understood as a symbolic reward; it tends to be relatively small. The big pay jumps occur by getting promoted to a job with a higher pay range. Contribution-based pay increases, on the other hand, reflect the results of a fundamental compensation review. Is this employee paid appropriately given the employee's impact on mission and business goals? Consequently, contribution-based pay increases can be very large and are often the only way pay levels get adjusted. Under many contribution-based systems, getting promoted has no direct impact on pay. All pay increases must be earned by demonstrating one's value to the mission. Promotions are simply an after-the-fact recognition that an employee's value and therefore pay level have moved to the next band.

Performance	Contribution
Compensation is based on projected value	*Compensation is based on demonstrated value*

In a performance-based system, compensation is based primarily on the level of the position, with small increases possible based on performance. When employees get promoted to a higher level position, their compensation is increased, often substantially, based on a projection that, in the new position, the employee will do work that is substantially more valuable to the organization. In contribution-based systems, employees receive compensation increases only after they have demonstrated that they have actually worked successfully at a higher level and can contribute in ways that are of greater value to the organization.

Performance	Contribution
Position-based	*Person-based*

Performance-based systems build off positions. The position defines the factors and standards for measuring performance. Positions define the pay range. The only way employees can escape the position is to get reassigned or promoted. Under contribution-based systems, the position becomes practically irrelevant. Employees can contribute very high on the scale or very low on the scale, regardless of their position. Contribution-based systems offer a structured way of moving to a person-based concept of personnel management.

Transforming HR Service Delivery 11

National Archives and Records Administration

Nathan Bailey
Glenn Sutton
Alexis Gray

Over the past decade, most federal HR organizations have been moving toward a much more strategic role, characterized by a focus on human capital, organizational strategy, and mission requirements, along with relatively less focus on processes, procedures, and HR transactions. At the same time, improvements in HR technology have made it possible to dramatically improve customer service while serving in a more strategic advisory role. Every federal organization needs to take a deep and unbiased look at what kinds of services it is providing customers, how it is delivering those services, what customers really want and need, and the technology that is supporting service delivery.

Inevitably, organizational priorities will change. Nonetheless, the need for HR organizations to provide strategic input on the organization's workforce and level of engagement, enterprise data related to human capital planning and organizational performance, and efficient recruiting and hiring support and outreach is here to stay. The challenge that most organizations face is coming up with ways to assume this strategic role while still finding time to fulfill operational responsibilities. Evaluating how your organization delivers HR services is critical and needs to be done not only thoughtfully but regularly as well.

The National Archives and Records Administration (NARA) has successfully made the transition from a transactional focus to a strategic business interest. NARA's approach involves a combination of process analysis and redesign; the selective application of HR technology; and the restructuring of HR roles and responsibilities. Today at NARA, the transformation is still underway.

The Situation in 2009

In 2009 the Human Capital Office at NARA was having a tough time. There had always been interest in jobs at the organization, but since the economic downturn, hundreds of people were applying for every job. Entry-level positions like archives technician were getting 500-plus applicants for each job vacancy that NARA posted on USAJOBS. Having a big applicant pool is usually great, but NARA was still using a manual, labor-intensive process for reviewing applicants.

It was the worst of both worlds: USAJOBS was making it easy for people to reuse application materials and apply for lots of federal jobs, but NARA's process was highly centralized, requiring that every inquiry from an applicant or hiring manager be routed through an HR staff member for a personalized response. This approach had worked well in a traditional paper-based environment, but it was not scalable to a modern online recruiting environment. Unfortunately, the disconnect NARA experienced among its personalized service-delivery model, its HR systems, and its approach to customer service is not unusual in the federal HR community.

From a service-delivery perspective, NARA's HR service delivery was "about as traditional an HR model as you can imagine," according to Analisa Archer, the Chief Human Capital Officer (CHCO) at NARA at the time. Analisa joined NARA in 2005 as NARA's first human capital management specialist when the agency's approach to HR focused on enforcing rules and offered limited flexibility.

Like many HR organizations, NARA's HR office was homegrown and had a staff with very long tenure. They had designed a very good HR office 25 years ago; however, their roles, service offerings, technology, and policies had not changed much over the years. The staff in the HR office realized that expectations about HR's role were evolving, but hadn't seen the opportunities or gotten traction around initiatives that could help them take on a more strategic role. Unfortunately, these challenges were starting to inhibit NARA's ability to function as a modern human-capital organization that could provide business value and guidance across the organization.

It is easy to understand why NARA wasn't pushing the envelope. Its approach to HR had worked for many years, especially when it was viewed through the lens of the traditional HR model. NARA's HR team helped managers hire new people into the organization and followed all the rules doing it. They managed and updated employee personnel records within their HR system. They administered benefits fairly and provided a great deal of information about those benefits to customers.

NARA was providing basic HR services with a very high degree of customer service. The HR team spent a lot of time working directly with managers, prospective employees, and benefits consumers, very often in face-to-face interactions. In the 1980s and 1990s, this approach made sense. The strategic demands on the HR department were limited and customers viewed HR as a transactional business. NARA's degree of customer service and face time with customers and stakeholders was highly valued.

HR Process Analysis and Redesign

NARA's HR management team was committed to transforming how and what services were offered. The team considered the kind of workforce that NARA would need in the coming years, how to provide outreach to target and recruit those individuals, which skill gaps turnover was likely to create, and the efficiency of recruiting and onboarding new staff members. HR as an organization didn't have the bandwidth or resources to fully address these issues, so the management team developed a plan to focus on four critical areas: (1) strengthening strategic human-capital planning, (2) improving the recruiting and hiring process, (3) improving the use of reporting and metrics for HR purposes, and (4) enhancing core-service delivery related to payroll, benefits, and personnel actions.

The team tackled recruitment first. HR improved some internal processes and policies for recruiting and hiring, and they began reaching out proactively to targeted audiences. They also began focusing much more explicitly on finding and recruiting a diverse pool of applicants. A workforce strategy branch was established to proactively conduct human-capital planning related to strategic workforce initiatives. This was a good start. However, HR faced challenges that involved business process and policy issues in combination with the use of outdated or nonexistent technology.

In 2009, a consulting firm was engaged to help address some of these challenges, focusing on evaluating NARA's HR service-delivery model and assessing technology options. The firm spent time getting to know the staff and meeting with the HR team in College Park, Maryland, as well as the operational HR staff that worked in St. Louis, Missouri. The consulting firm's efforts were initially directed to the question of whether NARA should adopt new HR technology, but they eventually led to process analysis and recommendations for improving all of the agency's HR processes, policies, and systems.

NARA conducted a series of meetings with subject matter experts (SMEs), stakeholders, and customers to get a sense of what was working well and where improvements were needed. HR's decision to train a critical eye on its own business processes and systems on a regular basis was the most powerful aspect of NARA's approach. In addition to critically analyzing its entire service-delivery model, NARA worked to institute policies, procedures, and systems that would enable the agency to review its HR performance in the future.

NARA's approach to this project involved several major steps. First, the agency conducted a review of all of its HR processes. The focus of this part of the project was the agency's business processes, policies, and standard operating procedures for the following:

- Personnel action processing

- Core payroll services and time reporting

- Staff acquisition, including recruitment, classification, diversity, job analysis, and entry-on-duty

- Organizational analysis and position management

- Employee and labor relations

- Performance management

- Reporting, including internal and external reporting as well as metrics.

For each of these functional areas, NARA held a series of interviews with key SMEs, stakeholders, and customers to examine or identify successes, challenges, flexibilities, regulatory issues, performance indicators, current baseline levels of performance, and target performance levels.

The second step of the project was to conduct a similar review of each of these functional areas in terms of HR systems and technology. NARA reviewed the systems and technology supporting each functional area to determine if a system was in place, whether that system was working well, its level of integration with other systems, and its ability to meet NARA's needs moving forward.

Following these reviews, the team developed recommendations for both short- and long-term changes to the way NARA performed its HR work and the systems used. The reviewers recommended new policies and policy revisions as well as new and revised business processes and standard operating procedures. NARA also developed recommendations regarding the technology that supported HR service delivery.

HR Technology

The front-end analysis and evaluation showed that many of NARA's issues stemmed from a lack of automated capabilities related to processing personnel actions, timekeeping, and recruiting and hiring. In addition to business process and policy concerns that both help and hinder HR service delivery, technology was recognized as a critical part of the conversation.

For example, moving to a more contemporary service-delivery model often means using technology like a human resources management system (HRMS). Also known as enterprise resource planning systems (ERPs), these systems are commonly used in the federal community. At their core, they are workflow management tools that integrate a lot of different HR data related to employee personnel information, payroll, and benefits. They generally allow users access to a database through a web-based or standalone application from their desktops. An HRMS also often provides self-service functionality where both employees and managers can view, initiate, and manage various activities and transactions, reducing the burden on HR professionals and improving engagement, accountability, and transparency with other systems users.

Besides self-service, the primary benefit of these systems is the automated workflow and integration between various HR functions where changes to an individual's records update related systems (e.g., a promotion automatically impacts an individual's pay and makes him/her eligible for different benefits). Although federal agencies may have useful HR-related tools and processes, if the systems aren't integrated to push and pull data from each other, duplicative and manual processes are necessary to generate useful, enterprise-level reporting. Agencies then must choose between spending a lot of time and money connecting their systems or creating high-workload, frustrating procedures that must be continually maintained to consolidate information.

With these considerations in mind, the HR management team made the recommendation to adopt a new, more modern human resources information technology (HRIT) system that was fully integrated with a payroll system. The team also recommended that NARA deploy a web-based time and attendance system, evaluate an enterprise reporting capability, and use an automated staffing tool to build and post jobs, rate and rank applicants, and perform other hiring actions. In addition, they suggested that NARA seriously consider implementing an automated entry-on-duty system that would help HR coordinate with new employees and facilitate onboarding.

As with many HR-related challenges, the combination of outdated or missing technology and inefficient policies and procedures can create significant and sometimes insurmountable issues for HR service delivery. For this reason, the NARA team also made numerous policy and business process recommendations that corresponded to and augmented many of the proposed systems improvements. Most of these process-related recommendations focused on rules for handling documents related to applications and new hires, new standards and procedures for position classification and management, permission for managers and employees to have access to self-service functionality within the new systems, policies for overpayments and leave advances, standards and policies for timecard review, and processes for eliminating all paper tracking of HR processes.

The team's analysis showed that the agency's then-current service provider could not meet the agency's requirements for a more modern HRIT system that was fully integrated with a payroll system. NARA decided to move forward with the migration to a different service provider.

NARA's developed a request for proposals (RFP) to provide to prospective providers. Operational capabilities demonstrations (OCDs) were scheduled, during which each provider walked through its system's basic functionality and addressed a number of different scenarios. Consulting with SMEs, the HR management team determined that the Department of the Interior's Interior Business Center (IBC) would best meet NARA's needs. That core HR system was deployed in April 2012, and the automated recruitment tracking and onboarding system (Workforce

Tracking and Transformation System/Entry on Duty System, WTTS/EODS) became operational in April 2013.

During the nearly two years it took for NARA to migrate its HR systems, the agency streamlined many HR processes, updated policies, and integrated a number of related but separate functions like training and development. As part of the migration to IBC, NARA deployed a fully integrated personnel, payroll, and enterprise reporting system that provides access to information across many of its HR systems and functions. WTTS/EODS is an especially valuable tracking and reporting tool that provides comprehensive information to HR staff and hiring managers on the status of recruiting actions and where prospective employees are in the transformation.

HR Roles and Responsibilities

Representatives from the HR management team have commented that they were surprised how supportive most stakeholders were throughout the process. This was largely a result of the significant amount of work the team put into providing change management and communications support throughout the process. NARA's philosophy was "early and often" when it came to getting people involved in the discussion about how the system should look, how their roles and responsibilities might change, and what the benefits (and risks) of the migration would be. Throughout most of the migration, NARA HR staff conducted monthly meetings with administrative officers and hiring managers to keep them in the loop, get their feedback, and gradually introduce them to likely shifts in their responsibilities and duties.

The human capital team worked closely with managers throughout the process to describe the opportunities that they would have, framing this transition as a way of empowering them and giving them authority and autonomy to initiate actions that were critical to them. NARA carefully reviewed its process for completing recruiting and hiring activities, focusing on where they could improve efficiency with automation, cross train HR staff, delegate responsibilities to hiring managers, and even consider delegating some of the work outside the organization (e.g., have OPM complete some of the more typical and standard NARA recruiting actions). The combination of technology and the service-delivery model created true efficiencies.

NARA also had to reconcile its model of customer service; the organization was spending so much time on certain aspects of its work that it was naturally making tradeoffs in other areas. Like most HR offices, NARA had several different customers, including current employees, prospective employees, hiring managers, leadership, and outside organizations like OPM and OMB. NARA had traditionally provided a very "high touch" interaction for almost all aspects for its work and interactions with these groups. This approach was no longer viable given the volume and complexity the agency's work had taken on in recent years. As part of this transformation effort, NARA worked to introduce greater standardization into work processes and formalize roles, responsibilities, and performance metrics associated with various functions. For example, NARA standardized many of its position descriptions (PDs); the HR office worked to reduce the need to develop customized PDs for every employee a hiring manager wanted to bring onboard.

The HR office also worked to establish the formal roles, responsibilities, and expected timelines for various aspects of the staffing process. The HR team continues to deploy and refine this strategy, monitoring timelines associated with the various phases of the staffing process and moving quickly to advise hiring managers of any bottlenecks and identify mitigation strategies (up to and including returning the hiring action to the manager until the manager is able to afford it the necessary attention). The deployment of WTTS/EODS has made this kind of tracking and accountability focus come to life.

NARA also made a conscious decision to reduce some of its internal audit and error-checking procedures related to recruiting and hiring to a more reasonable, yet completely adequate, level to save time and resources. The agency also established strict criteria for what applications to accept from prospective employees so staff didn't need to wait or coordinate as frequently with candidates who submitted duplicate or incomplete application packages. These kinds of decisions helped NARA free up resources so staff could prioritize where necessary and provide a very high level of service where it made sense, while streamlining efforts in other areas.

Managers and executives now have access to information. NARA has been working closely with them over time to ensure that the data they want is made available to them. With the new integrated system, managers have much greater visibility into where actions are in the recruitment process. They can view the status of the recruits in the hiring process, a task list of things they need to do to move various activities along in the HR workflow, and transactional data related to issues that can help them manage their staff, resources, and organizations more efficiently. Executives and managers now have data at their disposal and can more easily monitor the status of relevant HR-related activities.

NARA is still taking a number of things slowly. One is timekeeping. NARA had a very manual process for entering time, where employees submitted their time on various activities on a paper timesheet and then official timekeepers entered the information on their behalf into the system. NARA employees are now able to enter their time directly and have their managers approve timecards electronically. However, many of NARA's employees in the Federal Records Centers don't have regular access to a computer, so NARA will continue to evaluate the best time to put this functionality fully in place. In addition, many of the employee self-service functions and information have not been rolled out to the organization yet. NARA is working carefully and cautiously to determine how to introduce the best procedures to the workforce at large.

Benefits to the Agency

When asked if taking on this kind of transformation was the right decision and if it was ultimately worth it, NARA's HR management team responded that they believe that agencies have to go in this direction. A lot is expected of HR offices; to continue delivering even basic services and to ensure legal and regulatory compliance, HR organizations cannot be bogged down by time-consuming, highly manual transactional processes. These burdens were burying NARA in a huge backlog of recruiting and other personnel actions that were becoming increasingly difficult to manage.

In addition, the CHCO now sits on both the executive team and the management team at NARA, the two highest decision-making bodies in the organization. Given the combination of traditional HR responsibilities and the expectations to provide more strategic services, HR process, policy, and technology inefficiencies simply had to be addressed. Participating in strategic discussions and introducing business process and technology improvements have gone a long way toward putting NARA's HR organization on the right path.

One of the biggest payoffs for NARA resulting from the HR transformation is how much less paper (and the time spent moving that paper around) the organization is using. Prior to deployment, managers and HR had to route paperwork manually through the HR operations center in St. Louis, which could take 12 days. This meant almost two weeks of waiting and coordination before they could even start moving a candidate through the hiring process. In contrast, managers now have access to self-service functionality that completely eliminates the paper-based processes. Prospective employees are able to fill out most of their paperwork before showing up at NARA on their first day, eliminating the need for HR to enter the data manually. In fact, the organization has been able to cross-train and realign staff that previously performed manual data-entry activities to focus on more strategic, high-value aspects of the recruiting and hiring process.

NARA is also improving its hiring timeline, especially considering the new and labor-intensive requirements associated with OPM's Pathways program in addition to the increasing number of applicants that apply for every posted job (often 1000+).

Process improvements and the use of automated tools have enabled NARA to reduce its time-to-hire significantly.

NARA has been able to provide higher quality and more regular reporting as customers need it and to provide stakeholders with direct access to these reports. By eliminating paper-based manual processes and manual data entry, NARA has been able to free up time for HR staff to focus on critical but difficult issues like employee engagement. Improvements in technology have given HR staff the bandwidth to put programs, procedures, and evaluation strategies in place that will enhance engagement across the organization.

Lessons Learned

As other agencies consider similar changes in HR service delivery, they should take note of a few key lessons-learned from the NARA experience:

- *Work closely with stakeholders*, particularly customers, to evaluate their needs; prioritize those needs; install processes, procedures, and policies; and then manage expectations to allow HR to meet customer needs based on predefined standards.

- *Define roles and delegate*. HR doesn't have to do everything. Many HR departments are partnering across their organizations to define activities that individuals and organizations outside HR can do to support the HR mission. Embracing the employee- and manager-self-service philosophy can also free up critical resources.

- *Strive for fully integrated HR technology systems and services*. NARA moved to a new HR technology provider and is working to continuously improve and enhance its technology tools for HR and its customers.

- *Emphasize reporting capability*. One of the essential requirements for the human capital function to elevate its role is to develop its ability to advocate for the business value of human capital initiatives. Integrated systems, enterprise reporting, and the corresponding analysis and consulting are essential. The ability to create compelling and comprehensive reporting provides the foundation for HR to play a more strategic role in the organization.

- *Continue to improve.* Organizations always need to be looking for ways to improve business processes, change policies, reconfigure systems, and push vendors for new enhancements. It is imperative for organizations to install a structured and regular process that trains a critical eye on all aspects of HR service delivery to see where things can be improved, where needs have changed, where expectations aren't being met, and where things are going particularly well

Every federal organization needs to take a deep and unbiased look at what kinds of services it is providing customers, how it is delivering those services, what customers really want and need, and the technology that is supporting service delivery. NARA provides an excellent example of how to do these things in a systematic, thorough, and effective way.

When it comes to evaluating and implementing the resources and technology needed to get out in front of issues, NARA stands out as a model for other agencies based on its comprehensive and ongoing approach. NARA examined its entire HR lifecycle and was willing to challenge its staff to look for ways to improve how it conducted business, the policies it had in place, and the use of technology at the organization. NARA now has a powerful technical foundation of systems and business processes that will provide its capable HR staff the ability to take on a key strategic role for the organization.

HR Technology's Gold Standard 12

National Aeronautics and Space Administration

Nathan Bailey
Glenn Sutton
Alexis Gray

In 2006, NASA's human resources leaders had what some might consider a "happy problem." As part of an agency with a history and culture of technological innovation, they had developed and implemented an extensive set of HR technology systems to serve customers within the agency as well as a keenly interested external constituency: applicants for NASA's exciting and attractive mission-related positions.

NASA was in the process of implementing a comprehensive hiring solution, a benefits solution, workforce profile systems, and multiple Office of Personnel Management (OPM) initiatives and systems, including a human resources line of business (HRLOB) migration, a training system, a web-based system called "Employee Express" (an online service that allows NASA employees to make certain changes to their benefits and payroll information 24/7), and a thrift savings plan (TSP).

The agency was also still developing and using a variety of homegrown HR technology systems that were managed by different groups across the organization. Some of these 75 or so agency- and center-specific systems were valuable, but many were redundant and expensive to maintain; NASA's efforts to consolidate and integrate these disparate applications were becoming increasingly difficult.

NASA needed a unifying framework to provide consistent, integrated, and authoritative information that would meet stakeholder requirements while promoting ease of development, integration, and deployment of future enhancements. Ideally, this new architecture would not only incorporate best-of-breed technology, but would also let the systems share data easily and would create flexibility for adding, modifying, or removing systems without reinventing the wheel as NASA's needs changed over time. To meet these needs, NASA developed and successfully marketed a business case to create the human capital information environment (HCIE).

NASA's Technology Evolution

In contrast with many federal agencies, NASA has not taken a traditional approach to HR technology. Although the agency participates in the HRLOB, that system is only one part of NASA's larger enterprise system. NASA's entire architecture is designed to maintain, add, remove, and integrate various technologies easily across the agency as needs change. An important aspect of the agency's strategy related to HR technology development and deployment is the close collaboration between experienced, seasoned NASA HR information system (HRIS) developers and the HR community.

NASA's HR technology systems were not developed by the chief information officer (CIO), the internal IT organization, or contracting firms responding to RFPs. Instead, the development of these systems represents a tight-knit collaboration between HR functional teams working with NASA HRIS developers who have an in-depth understanding and knowledge of federal and NASA HR data, processes, functions, and regulations. This strategy helped NASA develop technically sound and high-impact solutions, placing front and center one of the most important aspects of change management: engaging users and experts in the design and development process early and often. NASA had to constantly integrate change management principles with its efforts to deploy new systems, focusing on advocating for technology-related changes, communicating the value and vision of those changes, gaining buy-in from users and experts, marketing and branding its efforts, providing effective training, and evaluating the effectiveness and impact of the systems.

One example of NASA's technology development and collaboration related to the electronic position description system (ePDS), which replaced a commercial product that was costing the agency about $1.3 million annually to maintain and operate—and was only partially compliant with federal classification standards. The internal NASA HRIS team, consisting of members from every NASA center along with two internal HRIS developers, developed and deployed the NASA ePDS in less than six months. Within a year of that deployment, over 95 percent of all NASA position descriptions were in the system. NASA's ePDS was recently acquired by the Interior Business Center (IBC) as an eventual service offering to its 48 customer agencies.

Not surprisingly, NASA did not develop its suite of technology systems overnight. In fact, the agency has experienced many of the challenges that all agencies face in getting buy-in from decision-makers and system users, making a good business case, finding personnel and funding resources, maintaining the systems, and staying on the cutting edge once systems are deployed.

NASA's Timeline

Until her retirement at the end of 2012, Candace Irwin was in charge of the HR technology group at NASA. For more than 20 years, Candace and her team were tasked with upgrading and consolidating NASA's systems as well as promoting the HR department as a strategic partner to the agency. When Candace joined NASA in 1991, the agency was just getting started on the web. Most of NASA's 10 centers had a website, but no branding. There was limited automation-related collaboration across the agency and each center maintained a robust HR office that provided high-touch, personalized customer service. Candace could quickly see the need and value associated with HR automation and knew that a group at the Johnson Space Center (JSC) headed up by Michael Stewart was already working on an automated system to support benefits administration. Although this system was supporting only JSC at the time, it ultimately formed the foundation for the eventual agencywide solutions Candace and Michael would partner to develop and deploy as part of the HCIE.

Beginning in 1995, NASA focused on public awareness branding through its NASA People website, which simultaneously educates the public about what it is like to work at NASA and provides its employees and HR staff easy access to HR information and tools. Candace continued her collaboration with Michael Stewart, and beginning in 1998, they worked to deploy NASA's first consolidated hiring website, called NASA Jobs. During this same time period, the government experienced significant budget cuts and NASA's HR office had to cut its numbers. NASA was simultaneously getting bogged down with an increasing workload in basic HR operations. (Think about how many high school students you know who want to be astronauts and you start to appreciate the magnitude of NASA's applicant pool, all of whom need to be processed and sent responses.) NASA wanted to provide its HR staff with help from automated systems. While the agency was able to develop and deploy an employee benefits system called NASA Employee Benefits System (NEBS), it was unable to get the funding needed for more agencywide systems and automation.

The situation began to shift in 2001, when NASA began to move away from center-specific systems. The NASA Personnel Payroll System (NPPS) was NASA's first HR enterprise system and its deployment spanned the entire agency. (In 2003 NASA migrated from NPPS to the federal personnel and payroll system, FPPS, at the Department of the Interior's IBC to manage its payroll information as part of the HRLOB initiative.)

NASA's next agencywide system was a time and attendance system called Webtads. As part of this deployment, NASA developed a centralized password system, which would become increasingly important with later integration efforts. Webtads was followed with a workforce information program called Workforce Information Cubes for NASA (WICN), which was built using IBM's Cognos enterprise reporting tool. After these systems were in place, NASA developed additional agencywide systems, including a hiring system (NASA STARS), a training system (SATERN), an entry-on-duty system, and a system to collect and manage employee contact information. These agencywide systems represented a big step toward consolidation and integration

By 2006, NASA had made a lot of progress in developing and deploying several agencywide systems. However, they were still operating with a mix of center and agencywide systems, and significant systems issues related to integration and consolidation needed to be addressed. At that point, NASA had 75 different HR applications in use, with minimal integration. NASA employees often had to search several systems to find answers to HR questions. A more significant issue for NASA was that the center-specific systems often had serious data integrity and consistency issues.

In parallel with the need for better integrated data, HR also needed to evolve into a more strategic partner role within the agency. With these goals in mind, NASA's HR leadership and staff began to develop a vision for what their data infrastructure solution should look like, namely, one that provides "an efficient and effective Human Capital Information Environment that delivers consistent, authoritative, near real-time information to stakeholders to enable informed decision-making." Initial requirements included keeping the data solution customer-driven, not IT-driven, while maintaining an adaptable IT infrastructure. HR leadership also wanted to move to one central repository for HR data, which would eliminate redundancies and costly maintenance.

With a clear vision to work from, Candace Irwin and her HR technology team began to build an initial business case and engage their Chief Human Capital Officer (CHCO), who was very supportive. The primary goals of the business case were to accomplish the following:

- Converge HC applications (functional and technical)

- Expand access to HC tools

- Increase capabilities of HC tools

- Interoperate the systems

- Justify the financial and personnel resources needed to achieve the HR technology vision.

NASA's HR technology team believed that these changes would result in (1) more reliable and widely available information, (2) a self-service environment to support managers, supervisors, and employees, (3) greater opportunities to improve HC processes, (4) better decision-making, and (5) improved enterprise and strategic planning. To build the business case, the team gathered hundreds of requirements from over 120 NASA leaders, managers, and program managers. They even brought in university professors to talk about the future of IT to help ensure that they would develop an innovative, forward-thinking solution.

Using all this information, Candace and her team put together a business case that detailed a clear plan for what they needed, supported by a comprehensive cost/benefit analysis. Throughout the process they made sure to engage leadership; and once NASA leaders were excited about the project, it became much easier to get the right people to direct resources toward it.

Human Capital Information Environment

So what does the HCIE look like? Broadly, it's an authoritative data warehouse that integrates with agency automation tools and systems that support the full HR lifecycle; this information is presented through a robust HR portal. Instead of duplicative programs and redundant data marts with conflicting information, NASA now has one data warehouse with carefully vetted human capital data fields that all other programs and systems access. This keeps data consistent across all programs and systems. Even better, NASA is able to use a "plug and play" approach to its human capital systems; new systems can be added or removed with ease, since each is tied to only the data warehouse rather than to each other. More importantly, NASA has created a single and comprehensive portal to the system that provides tailored access to users across the organization (Figure 12-1).

To borrow NASA's metaphor for the HCIE, think of the HC systems as the spokes of a wheel with the data warehouse as the hub and the HR portal as the presentation layer. Any spoke can be replaced with another spoke, and none of the other

NASA's Human Resources Portal

FIGURE 12-1

spokes will be affected. For example, NASA's participation in the HRLOB initiative through its use of the federal personnel and payroll system (FPPS) does not constrain the HCIE. Instead, FPPS functions as just one more data feed that plugs into the data infrastructure, along with data from NASA's competency management system, succession planning system, and recruitment and hiring systems.

While the HCIE and its systems are designed to meet individual, organizational, and strategic needs, in keeping with NASA's focus on customer service, they also focus on the user experience. During the same time period that NASA was building the HCIE, the agency continued to develop agencywide systems that could be integrated with it, including an awards system, a classification system, a data dictionary, and a mentoring program. Today, the HCIE comprises 31 integrated systems.

NASA has also taken steps to provide authoritative information for decision-making and to improve operational efficiency. For example, NASA makes the HCIE available to all employees through a single point of access on their desktops called the HR portal. With an easily accessible, self-service portal, employees can avoid waiting times, update personal information, gain easy access to routine information (e.g., healthcare plans), and get immediate responses to requests for information. Leaders and other decision-makers can also access dashboards and reporting, and managers can view workforce alignment data, make vacancy projections, manage training requests, and initiate recruitment actions.

The following are the core systems that make up NASA's HCIE (seven of which IBC has acquired to include as part of its offerings to other federal agencies):

- *System for administration, training, and educational resources for NASA (SATERN).* SATERN is NASA's learning management system. It provides online career development materials like individual development plans as well as a host of web-based training materials, including online courses, training simulations, and test preparation for certification exams. NASA recently upgraded the platform to enable its workforce to access training resources in a more collaborative environment that includes mobile devices. Using SATERN, employees can access training materials, including e-books, videos, and online courses, on their iPhones or iPads in a mobile format.

- *Federal employees benefits system (FEBS).* FEBS is a NASA-developed, comprehensive employee benefits statement that is available online 24/7 through Employee Express. The system provides current personal benefits information based on each employee's personal elections, employment record, and income (the embedded calculations and data are updated weekly). FEBS was originally developed by internal NASA benefits specialists and programmers who conceived and developed it as the NASA employee benefits system (NEBS). NASA's supporting federal shared services center, DOI's IBC, adopted the system and now provides it to NASA and other federal agencies. In 2004, NEBS was cited in OMB's report to Congress on eGOV as the major NASA eGOV accomplishment for the previous year. Recurring estimated cost and benefits staff savings are in excess of $650,000 per year as a result of customer self-service and staff reduction.

- *NASA automated awards system (NAAS).* NAAS is a web-based application that provides the interfaces and automated processes to initiate, review, approve, and monitor award submissions for both NASA-wide and local center awards. NASA developed the application to consolidate and unify all award processing into a single agencywide management system. The application incorporates workflow automation and the functionality to manage multiple award types such as NASA honor awards, monetary and time-off awards, and center-specific awards.

- *NASA's competency management system (CMS).* CMS is used to categorize, identify, measure, and forecast NASA's corporate knowledge base. CMS allows the agency to collect, manage, and report on the workforce competencies as they relate to people, positions, and projects. By providing NASA with information on workforce knowledge, skills, and expertise that can be aligned to the agency's mission through the budget process, CMS enables NASA to build expertise in targeted knowledge areas.

- *NASA organization profile system (NOPS).* NOPS is a NASA-developed, online, 11-page organization summary report that provides supervisors and key staff comprehensive statistics and workforce indicators for their organization. Users may view comparative data on all organizations along with specific, by-name employee information on members of their own organization. NOPS has an estimated cost avoidance and staff savings in excess of $450,000 per year as a result of customer self-service and staff redeployment. OPM has cited NOPS as an agency best practice in its annual report to federal agencies.

- *NASA employee orientation website.* For new, transferring, and detailed NASA employees, the NASA employee orientation website provides the information, forms, contacts, and checklists they need to begin working at their new NASA duty station. The website is the also the entry point for NASA's entry-on-duty system (EODS), which allows new personnel to complete required forms and documentation in real-time.

- *Workforce transformation and tracking system (WTTS).* WTTS is a NASA-developed, web-based case management tool used to manage, track, and report on prospective hiring actions, moves, and losses. WTTS is an essential component of civil servant identity management. The system also supports buyouts, recruiting, drug testing, use of NASA workforce flexibilities, and other special programs. In 2008, NASA provided WTTS to DOI's IBC, which now provides the system to its customer agencies.

- *Emergency notification system (ENS).* ENS is an agency-wide application that provides NASA unparalleled critical-communications capabilities, enhancing emergency response and employee safety. ENS provides NASA the ability to send messages, both agency- and center-related, to personnel in the event of an emergency or emerging situation at a NASA facility. Notifications can be delivered via multiple communication devices (e.g., e-mail, text, cellular, home/office phone numbers). The system gives NASA personnel the ability to respond to notifications and provide their safety status. It also offers NASA the ability to track and report on employee safety during an event.

- *Employee emergency contacts system (EECS).* EECS system is a NASA-developed, web-based tool used to record, track, and report individual employees' emergency contact information. The employee maintains the information online with secure self-service access and reporting to the management chain and key staff. EECS is available to employees 24/7 through Employee Express. The system has had significant impact on employee safety and welfare. DOI's IBC now provides the system to its customer agencies.

- *Entry-on-duty system (EODS).* EODS is a NASA-developed, web-based tool used for onboarding NASA employees. The system provides automated entry-on-duty forms completion, processing, and review. In 2006, the companion tool, the NASA employee orientation website, was recognized by the Federal Webmasters Forum as the best federal website for a specialized audience.

- *Human capital executive dashboards.* These dashboards provide an easy, visually friendly display of key performance indicators (KPIs) to aid leaders and key stakeholders in decision-making. Each dashboard provides subviews for workforce alignment (e.g., workforce size, skills, composition), workforce readiness (e.g., hiring, training, competency gaps), and workforce sustainability (e.g., NASA's employee profile as related to long-term viability for the agency). Each subview displays summarized data and trend analysis for each KPI.

- *Human resources messaging system (HRMES).* This communication tool uses filters to provide HR messages targeted to each individual employee's needs. For example, the system sends a reminder when an employee's project management certification is about to expire. Messages are sent to employee email accounts and through the HR portal.

- *STARS.* NASA's automated staffing and recruitment system, STARS is integrated into NASA's human resources portal. This system provides a dashboard of vacancy data, a vacancy announcement builder, a vacancy announcement library, a requisition library, and candidate contact information. STARS also is fully integrated with OPM's USAJOBS website. Much of the power behind STARS comes from Resumix, automated resume scanning software that provides NASA's hiring managers with a skills assessment for job applicants based on the content of their resumes. This tool is useful for evaluating scientific and technical positions and streamlines the application process; applicants need only submit a resume.

- *NASA People.* NASA's site for job seekers, retirees, and the public (Figure 12-2), NASA People provides information about jobs, benefits, retirement information, and what it is like to work for NASA. It also provides extensive information for employees and HR professional regarding NASA's leadership development programs, its supplemental classification system, and its human capital program.

Return on Investment

NASA has benefited tremendously from its focus on integrated, user-friendly technology. For example, NASA uses its

FIGURE 12-2

NASA People

automated systems in combination with employee self-service to process 20,000 awards and hold 275,000 online classes each year. Using the same approach, the agency processed 57,190 applicants through NASA's automated staffing and recruitment system in 2010. In addition to managing high volumes of employee-related actions, NASA is experiencing other efficiencies. Before automation, the average number of days to hire was 150; it is now 91. NASA also saves $4 million each year by eliminating manual rating panels and another $5 million each year because its streamlined onboarding process reduces time-to-productivity for new employees.

NASA has even seen an increase in employee satisfaction. Ninety-four percent of new employees are satisfied with the hiring process, and employees appreciate the convenience of having a single sign-in for all HR matters. Managers are also pleased with improved employee selection: 85 percent of managers say that applicant referrals have the talent required.

NASA's HR department is considered a strategic partner in NASA decision-making. By automating so many transactional functions, NASA has freed its employees from administrative work, which allows them to focus on more engaging, higher impact functions like consulting and strategic planning.

With such remarkable outcomes, it's no surprise that HCIE applications have won seven exceptional software awards, been named the best federal website for specialized audiences, and been recognized in three annual OMB reports to Congress on e-Gov. NASA worked hard to make these accomplishments and didn't stop once HCIE was deployed. A working group is dedicated to reviewing HCIE and related topics. For example, when NASA migrated its data to HCIE, in some instances centers needed to retain their data marts because their work required specialized data. NASA continues to work to ensure that there are no redundant fields between those data marts and HCIE. The agency also continues to develop new systems (e.g., a new performance management tool called SPACE) and revamp current systems, recently relaunching improved versions of both NASA STARS and NASA People.

Change Management at the Department of Labor

While NASA may be at the front of the pack in terms of technological innovation, it isn't the only federal agency to embrace technology. The Department of Labor (DOL) is in the process of its own migration to an HRLOB shared-service center and has been an HR technology trailblazer since the deployment of its version of PeopleSoft (called PeoplePower at DOL) in 1999.

One area where DOL pushes the envelope is change management for new technology deployments. Alvin (Chip) Black, Director of the Office of HR Systems at DOL, has worked very closely with the many DOL subject matter experts (SMEs) as well as the CIO's office, where he partners with an experienced IT project manager, Albert (Al) Sloane, who is the director at Benefits.gov. Both Chip and Al acknowledge that even the best system isn't likely to be a success without proper buy-in from the workforce. As a result, the DOL team has emphasized the need to get the word out on the system early and often, focusing on organizational assessment, systems and process improvement discussions, strategic communication development and distribution, and training and development initiatives. As part of the vendor selection and planning stages of the project, Chip and Al have engaged hundreds of SMEs and stakeholders to identify features, challenges, and strategies for addressing those challenges.

Beyond engaging their SMEs, Chip and Al have also made sure they are engaging the rest of the workforce through a number of activities, including the following:

- *Change readiness assessment.* DOL conducted surveys and interviews with key stakeholders to understand the perceived level of organizational support for the migration, the extent to which the migration was viewed as beneficial, and the preferred methods and messages for future project-related communication.

- *Communication and change management plan.* The team developed a project communication and change management plan to identify an approval workflow, key messages, key stakeholders, and the various communication vehicles available to disseminate project-related information.

These vehicles include project newsletters, a project website, project fact sheets, and targeted "What you need to know" FAQs.

- *Project branding.* To provide a clear and consistent look, feel, and message to all project-related communications, the DOL team developed a branding and style guide, complete with a project color scheme, project dictionary, logo, and templates for various communication vehicles (e.g., reports, PowerPoint briefings, newsletters).

- *Training plan.* DOL has developed a training plan to complement the training and materials offered by Treasury. The training plan identifies key staff members, training format and length, and associated roles and responsibilities of those staff members (e.g., system power users, trainers, project champions, content developers); DOL will also be working over the coming year to develop additional custom content and materials to augment what is available from Treasury. As part of this effort, the DOL team will offer a variety of training types (e.g., web-based, classroom, town hall) and materials to meet the specific needs across DOL stakeholders.

NASA also regularly takes a hard look at its business processes and policies, and in some cases has pushed back a bit on governmentwide guidelines to find ways to meet needs more effectively. For example, when processing job applicants, NASA found that it was more efficient to perform its rating process first and then process minimum qualifications, so the agency negotiated with OPM to make that change.

Lessons Learned

Without good technology and a solid long-term vision of how that technology will support the organization, it is difficult for federal agencies to get out from under the burdens of traditional HR responsibilities to become true strategic partners. Based on the NASA experience, here are some key considerations in making technology innovation in HR environments successful:

- *Plan, evaluate, implement, repeat.* It is imperative that federal organizations train a critical eye on themselves to evaluate the current state of their technology, their short- and long-term needs, and strategies for reaching their goals. At the same time, they need to pay attention to new IT developments and assess how new options (e.g., social media) may or may not benefit them. This process needs to be continual, and it doesn't end when an HRLOB migration takes place. NASA truly excels at sustaining this process. The organization is constantly evaluating its needs, new technology trends, and the performance and value of deployed systems to ensure that resources are spent wisely and that it remains on the leading edge of HR technology in government.

- *Empower employees and managers.* Employee and manager self-service was a major driver for development of the NASA HCIE. Access to information and the ability of employees and managers to do the work themselves were primary drivers of NASA's technology development and deployment efforts. Stakeholders outside HR could initiate personnel actions and processes and then monitor the status of those activities. This is especially critical as part of the recruiting and hiring process. Although training, mentoring, and effective policies need to go along with this shift, enabling self-service is one of the best ways for HR to reduce some of its burden and shift focus to other, higher value activities.

- *Make a strong business case.* Sometimes it takes more resources—whether those resources will be used to hire more staff, train existing staff, deploy new systems, upgrade existing systems, or augment marketing and outreach efforts. More than ever, organizations need to understand the business case for allocating additional resources. NASA went to great lengths to describe the benefits, risks, and return on investment of the HCIE and to make its case in terms of utility to the organization.

- *Manage change systematically and deliberately.* Any major change within an organization, whether it relates to structure, leadership, objectives, or technology, takes a lot of work. Both NASA and DOL have spent considerable resources communicating, marketing, establishing buy-in, and training their organizations on new technology systems. A key element for both organizations was including experts and stakeholders across the organization at every step of the design, development, and deployment of new systems. Keeping stakeholders engaged and providing tailored information in a variety of formats is critical to any major change initiative, especially those that transform technology across an organization.

- *Go beyond the HRLOB.* NASA has created a highly flexible technology infrastructure of which IBC components are one part. As a result, the agency can easily add to, replace, modify, and most important, integrate different technologies as needs change. Early planning and a forward-looking perspective are critical to ensure that an organization's technology will support its current and future model of service delivery as needs change. NASA has partnered with IBC to provide access to NASA-developed HR solutions, including seven different HRIS applications, so that IBC can offer these solutions to its other client organizations.

NASA has succeeded in becoming the "gold standard" for human capital technology in the federal government. The agency's HCIE is strategic, comprehensive, fully integrated, customer-oriented, and supported by a strong business case. Furthermore, because of the disciplines and practices ingrained in the fabric of NASA's systems development process, the HCIE is positioned to grow and evolve as technologies and agency needs continue to change.

HR Customer and Strategic Services

National Institutes of Health

Glenn Sutton
Cristina Wilcox

National Institutes of Health (NIH) comprises institutes and centers (ICs) that focus on a variety of medical research agendas in support of the overall mission "to seek fundamental knowledge about the nature and behavior of living systems and the application of that knowledge to enhance health, lengthen life, and reduce the burdens of illness and disability." NIH is the largest source of medical research funding in the world, with scientists doing research for NIH at universities, medical schools, and other institutions throughout the world.

NIH headquarters, in Bethesda, Maryland, houses researchers, the NIH clinical center, and the Office of the Director. Although the ICs operate fairly independently, the Office of the Director is responsible for NIH-wide policy and processes, strategic planning for the agency as a whole, and coordination of research activities across all ICs. The Office of Human Resources (OHR) falls under the Office of the Director, functioning as a centralized unit that provides client services, workforce-relations support, and strategic human capital programs to NIH headquarters and all ICs.

With a unique and specialized mission and workforce within the federal government, NIH faces distinct human capital challenges in recruiting and developing employees. One pervasive challenge across federal HR organizations is balancing quick, responsive operational HR service delivery with proactive strategic human capital advisory services. NIH has successfully built and maintains an organization that achieves excellent operational outcomes, provides valuable strategic analysis and guidance, and upholds a culture of customer service that fully supports the mission of NIH headquarters and the ICs.

The Evolution of HR at NIH

Over the past 10 years, NIH has undergone various cycles of decentralization and centralization of HR operations. In 2003, the Department of Health and Human Services (HHS) implemented an initiative to consolidate all HR operations at the HHS level. This initiative sought to standardize, centralize, and improve HR business processes throughout the department by establishing five HR shared-service centers (SSCs) in Atlanta, Baltimore, Rockville, NIH, and the Indian Health Service (IHS). The department required significant staff reductions in the HR SSCs, which were to be offset by the development and deployment of new automated systems.

Prior to the consolidation initiative, NIH had 25 HR offices— nearly one for each IC. Ultimately, NIH and IHS were exempted from consolidating their HR operations under the HHS SSC. However, NIH was required to centralize its HR operations in its Office of Human Resources. As part of this transition, NIH was required to reduce its HR staff from about 450 FTEs (full-time equivalents) to a maximum of 256 FTEs within two years. This initial consolidation left NIH with an inadequate level of HR support.

A transition committee comprising OHR and IC representatives was formed under OHR's leadership to design and implement the transition within the footprint required by HHS. Recognizing the need for more information regarding customer expectations and needs, as well as best practices, NIH leadership contracted with the National Academy for Public Administration (NAPA) to hold internal focus groups and perform benchmarking.

NIH and OHR adopted an organizational design aimed at balancing the need to consolidate HR operations with the need to foster effective client relationships. The new centralized structure combined administrative support centers (to handle functions in which efficiency and process are critical), centers of expertise (where specialized knowledge serves the whole community in developing policies, resources, and best practices), and business partnerships (consultative services to address any unique needs of individual ICs). OHR now comprises five divisions and two additional organizations under associate directors:

- Client Services Division

- Compensation and Senior/Scientific Employment Division

- HR Systems, Analytics and Information Division

- Workforce Relations Division

- Workforce Support and Development Division

- Associate Director for Administrative Management

- Personnel Policy and Accountability Group.

When the reorganization went into effect, the ICs felt the impact of the foundational and resource shifts almost immediately. The new model better supported NIH as a corporate entity; for example, eventually this model allowed strategic recruiting for NIH rather than just individual ICs. It also created a broader knowledge base within HR and enhanced consistency in policies and processes. However, it meant that the individual ICs no longer had HR employees as direct reports. Many of the former HR staff had been moved from their physical locations in the ICs to HR hubs, some off campus. Moreover, veteran HR staff, whose institutional knowledge and experience were invaluable, were lost in the mandated staff reductions. Some workers retired earlier than planned; others accepted new jobs outside the HR field. Consequently, NIH experienced a significant decrease in the quality of HR services, especially those provided directly to clients. Initially, complaints were high and morale was low.

The results of the NAPA study and follow-on efforts by OHR gave NIH senior leadership support to justify 60+ additional FTEs in 2005 and 22 additional FTEs in 2006. By 2006, substantial progress had been made in the restaffing effort. However, gaps in service delivery still needed to be addressed on a larger scale. First, OHR needed to be able to provide a consistent high level of operational and strategic customer service to the ICs, including hiring, classification, employee relations, and day-to-day operations. As a next step, OHR wanted to function as a strategic entity to provide human capital planning, analysis, and advisory services to NIH leadership and across the organization.

Many HR offices across the federal government face similar challenges and have similar goals. They strive to provide excellent operational services and function as a strategic advisory resource with leadership and organizationwide. How is it possible to do both effectively when an HR office faces so many demands on its time and resources? Where does the HR office start, and how does it maintain a high level of service going forward? It is not easy to play both roles successfully, but NIH has been able to do so. This transformation did not happen overnight; it took a consistent, focused effort that was supported by leadership and bolstered by contributions from employees at multiple levels throughout the organization.

Customer-Focused Strategic and Operational Support

In 2012, Phil Lenowitz, Deputy Director of Human Resources, described the strategies that he and Chris Major, Director of Human Resources, used to achieve NIH's successful transformation of the strategic and operational HR organization. After 60+ new staff were hired in a three-month period, Phil and Chris focused on the ICs' immediate functional needs: "hiring, classification, recruitment, pay setting, all the day to day operations, employee relations…we built that up first because that's where the clamoring was." This initial push toward building a solid foundation for effective operational services was called the

Austin project (drawing inspiration from Steve Austin, the main character of the 1970s television show *The Six Million Dollar Man*). As Phil explained, we wanted to build a "better, stronger, faster" model for HR service delivery.

HR leaders gathered feedback from colleagues across NIH—executives, senior IC leaders, scientists and researchers, and administrative staff. Through this extensive outreach effort, HR identified three main steps that could be taken to address some of the common themes expressed by its customers:

- *Colocation*. The most salient change in the shift from independent HR offices to a consolidated HR organization was the loss of "face time" between HR specialists and institute staff. HR leaders recognized the importance of striking a balance between complete consolidation and complete IC independence. Some ICs expressed more of a need for on-site HR staff. HR agreed that if the ICs requested colocation and were willing to provide the space, HR would provide the people. ICs had the flexibility to request colocated staff full-time or on a rotational basis. This blended approach took the unique needs of each customer organization into account rather than trying to apply a one-size-fits-all solution.

  Phil explains that "anybody [in HR] who deals with the institutes and centers is supposed to spend at least one day per quarter with their customers...go into a lab and spend the day with a lab chief, or sit in on a scientific meeting to see what kinds of things they're dealing with. Our staff is more in touch with the mission, and the managers recognize the people. It's about the relationship. If you have good relationships with the people you service, you're going to do better at your job and they're going to be happier."

- *Organization*. With the ICs' participation, HR leaders came up with a modified structure for the Client Services Division (CSD). The new structure added two deputy directors and an associate director under the

CSD director. The deputy directors split supervisory duties for the ten branches that provided HR services to the ICs; IC representatives had input into the selection of the deputy directors as well as leaders in the CSD branches. The associate director supervised areas such as the delegated examining unit, the classification unit, internal operations, and the commissioned corps. The additional level of supervision freed up more time for individual branch chiefs to spend with the ICs, increasing coordination, consistency, and consultation across branches. According to Chris Major, director of OHR, this structure worked quite well: "The new CSD organization more efficiently allocated the senior level resources. This allowed the CSD leadership to think strategically by spreading operational decisions among seasoned leaders. It enabled CSD to drive accountability and customer service to the next level. And importantly, it provided the impetus for staff to look at the metrics that measured their work, a motivating factor resulting in greater productivity."

- *Accountability*. Findings from the Austin project suggested a need for increased accountability for customer service. CSD began focusing on concrete ways to build a customer service culture. One example was revision of the performance elements in CSD performance plans. Branch chiefs and HR specialists each have a performance element that measures customer service. However, instead of being rated by their immediate supervisors within CSD, the institute staff members who the branch chiefs or specialists serve are responsible for rating customer service. This gives ICs direct input into performance appraisal and ensures that CSD staff are directly accountable to their customers in a meaningful way. It also builds mutual accountability by putting the onus on ICs to raise any concerns about customer service.

Multiple factors contributed to the success of the Austin project, which was a large-scale undertaking that resulted in substantial improvements to service delivery. It may seem obvious that the first step toward improving customer service is to ask your customers what they need; however, when the customers are distributed across 27 ICs and cover a broad range of functions, this is quite a task. Where feedback on customer needs differed, OHR tailored its response and subsequent actions.

The reorganization went beyond moving employees and resources around. Building in accountability was an important factor, but the HR leaders also made a point of ensuring that employees were grounded in essential HR competencies through training and development. Instilling a customer service culture was important, but employees also needed to have the knowledge and expertise to know *how* to serve their customers most effectively. For example, if an HR specialist had to deny a manager's hiring request because of regulatory constraints, it was important that the specialist be able to offer alternatives to reach a solution that worked for everyone.

The key to the success of the renewed OHR was the development of a strong leadership team. Each division director and associate director became not only the leader of his or her organization, but also a steward of OHR. The ability of the members of this team to recognize the needs of the entire organization—and to be global in their thinking—was vital to building a great organization. Also key to building capacity in OHR were implementing new ideas, taking carefully considered risks, and engaging in robust debate that not only allowed, but demanded, that all views on a subject be discussed and subject to critical analysis and scrutiny. Innovation was possible only because of the characteristics of this team. Chris notes that "putting the right people on the bus was foremost as we built our team. We knew that with the right people, we would be able to become more than a service provider. OHR would be become integral to the NIH mission."

The initial success of the Austin project gave OHR the momentum to continue pushing toward further improvement. To bolster and expand the customer service culture it had been building, OHR brought in a new leader for the Client Services Division, Valerie Gill. Valerie's vision for CSD aligned with this new direction. Three phrases guided her approach to HR service delivery:

"Engage the team. Improve the process. Thrill the customer." Valerie introduced numerous initiatives that demonstrated her commitment to putting these phrases into practice.

Valerie recognized the need for creativity in her organization and the importance of providing ongoing support for her employees' successful ideas. One of the branch chiefs came up with the idea of holding a strategic recruitment meeting (SRM) for the ICs she serviced; the positive results led to NIH-wide implementation of the meetings. Before the SRMs became part of the CSD process, a manager would request a hire and the HR specialist would create and post a job announcement based on the information the manager included in the request. The strategic recruitment meetings involve an investment of time up front to identify the key characteristics of the specific hiring needs. When an IC requests a hire, the HR specialist meets with the selecting official, the administrative officer from the IC, and any other relevant stakeholders. As Phil explains, "They talk about the process that will follow, what we'll need the manager and the administrative officer to do, what HR will do, and what the time frame is. That's helpful. But the important part is that we go to the manager and we say, 'What is it you're looking for? Tell us what the ideal candidate looks like.'"

The HR specialist asks a series of targeted questions to elicit as much information as possible about the customer's needs for a candidate. For example:

- Are you looking for a particular specialty within this scientific area (e.g., a general chemist vs. a chemist with a specialized focus or research background)?

- Where might we be able to find people with this skill set?

- What organizations might be good to recruit from, keeping in mind the overarching NIH goal of achieving diversity in our workforce?

- What types of recruitment benefits would help you appeal to this type of candidate (e.g., recruitment bonus, student loan repayment)?

The manager gains a realistic overview of the time frame and his or her role in the process, while the HR specialist gains detailed information about the customer's needs. The SRM process has numerous benefits. First, the time invested up front saves substantial time later in the process. The meeting educates the customer on his/her responsibilities so that time frames do not slip because the customer is unsure what to do. It also provides a level of accountability for the HR specialist. The specialist tells the customer exactly what to expect, and then the specialist is responsible for delivering on those expectations. The meeting also reinforces the relationship between the customer and the HR team. Both sides come to the table to lay out the plan, and potential obstacles to the recruitment process are addressed up front. The SRM worked so well for NIH OHR that the CSD branch chief who envisioned the idea traveled to conferences and other agencies to speak about its benefits and share lessons learned from its implementation at NIH.

Valerie also led CSD staff through a pilot of an HR clinic program—another idea from a branch chief who planned it for a small group of ICs. Valerie explains that "the clinic was another way for us to provide value to our customers; educate them on the OHR services available to them; help them understand their role in ensuring the success of the recruitment and other OHR process; address any questions or suggestions they may have to enhance the OHR program and strengthen our relationship with them." The idea was so well-received that the clinic was opened to all of NIH.

The first HR clinic was an all-day event at a conference center where participants could choose from 20 sessions on 13 HR topics, including benefits, retirement planning, classification, hiring authority requirements and flexibilities, and administrative matters. HR staff worked collaboratively with their customers while planning the event by collecting survey feedback on topics of interest. On the day of the event, HR staff members were available between sessions at tables representing various branches and initiatives to talk one-on-one with IC attendees. The clinic provided the opportunity for HR staff to engage with their customers in person and for administrative professionals from different ICs to network with one another. Plans for the next NIH-wide HR clinic are now underway.

As IC needs change—whether driven by research priorities, resources, leadership change, or other factors—HR must adapt to continue effectively meeting needs. CSD's strong customer service culture enables HR to identify opportunities for improvement before potential issues escalate. For example, when a need for closer working relationships between CSD and the NIH clinical center emerged, CSD held facilitated meetings with the center's senior leadership and the CSD leader to clarify roles, responsibilities, and expectations. As Phil notes: "They got to work together face to face and got to know each other. We've done the same thing with the National Cancer Institute and the National Eye Institute. Each one is a little different because it caters to the needs of that particular institute. They've developed a variety of tools that, while they were developed with one institute, they can use it elsewhere as these partnerships grow."

Balancing NIH's overarching strategic direction with the diverse needs of individual ICs is no easy task; conflicts and challenges are bound to arise. One of the ongoing general challenges that HR leaders face is being available to lead successful operational HR and weigh in on escalated HR cases while still finding the time to lead the proactive efforts in strategic planning. With the foundation of customer-focused HR service delivery in place, it was important to NIH's human capital leaders not to lose focus on opportunities for further improvement.

Strategic Human Capital Planning, Analysis, and Advisory Services

Although the initial focus of the HR transformation was to address NIH's immediate operational needs, it was important to HR leaders to move toward a more strategic model where they were also able to provide valuable analysis and advisory services. The director and deputy director started by taking opportunities to provide strategic advice and guidance as they arose, demonstrating the added value they could bring to the organization beyond day-to-day HR services. For example, the HR team led a study of compensation for scientific and medical staff that was critical in enabling NIH to recruit top talent. When NIH was facing the possibility of a furlough, HR took the lead in analyzing the estimated impact, identifying essential personnel, and laying out a plan to deal with the situation.

The director of NIH started calling on Chris, Phil, and their staff for strategic advice and service more frequently. "As we were able to deliver the day-to-day services to the ICs, senior leaders gained confidence in our ability to expand our portfolio," says Chris. "As difficult tasks came into NIH, OHR was called upon to deliver. This caused us to look at our business in a different way and to alter our thinking. We began anticipating what our senior leaders needed and were delivering more than we promised instead of promising more than we could deliver. We were no longer only an operations organization. We were being integrated into the senior leadership of NIH. And resources needed to be allocated appropriately to meet those requirements."

Chris and Phil knew that with the complexity of the organization and the variety of NIH stakeholders, they could always expect something to be coming down the pipeline that would have an impact on human capital, whether it be a new mandate from HHS, an executive order, or an internal shift in priorities. Phil explains that they "needed a way to respond to this; not necessarily the experts, but the people who can figure out what we need to do, get to the experts, and coordinate these projects." They created a strategic initiatives group (SIG) to help HR move from an ad hoc, reactive strategic advisory model to a model that was more organized, yet agile enough to adapt to different priorities as they emerged. Creation of the SIG demonstrates a continuation of Chris and Phil's deliberate effort to maximize the value of HR's resources and services.

The SIG is currently made up of a small group of management analysts. Chris and Phil manage the group, but it generally functions as a self-directed work team. The group's projects vary in topic, scope, and urgency. The SIG can be called upon to spring into action when a quick-turnaround request comes down from the director's office, or it can be asked to propose a strategic solution to an ongoing challenge internally where members are able to devote more time and resources to planning and piloting the program. Along with having direct access to the HR director and deputy director, this group is empowered to work directly with the appropriate high-level contacts on any given project or initiative. This enables the SIG to function independently and to gather the information it needs to move quickly and efficiently.

One example of a large-scale SIG initiative is the five-star executive recruitment program. A SIG member (who was a presidential management fellow) saw an opportunity to improve the executive recruitment process by more fully integrating HR coordination with the Office of the Director. Originally, staff from that office would coordinate visits for interviewing executives, with HR involved at various points in the process. This employee proposed that HR take ownership of the entire process to make it a smoother operation from beginning to end. Since HR staff were already involved in posting the announcements and facilitating the selection of candidates to interview, it made sense for them to remain a consistent point of contact all the way through to the employee's onboarding.

The executive recruitment program has proven beneficial to the director, the selecting organizations, and the candidates. OHR's coordination of the process end-to-end builds a relationship with new executives from the beginning, demonstrating that HR is an organization that is attuned to its customers and ready to go the extra mile to support them.

The SIG has been extremely valuable in responding to HR issues, but its members are hardly the only employees who contribute to strategic human capital planning and analysis at NIH. OHR has access to a wealth of HR data through the workflow information tracking system (WITS). The system's original purpose was to track hiring actions to figure out where they are in the process and how long it takes to complete each step. Since the system was built, its usage has expanded both within and outside OHR. The HR Systems, Analytics, and Information Division (HR SAID) uses the information from this system to support a data-driven approach to both the operational and strategic functions.

For example, an IC decided not to allocate any of its annual budget to giving performance awards one year. HR SAID was able to analyze the turnover rates in this IC and determine that they were not significantly different from turnover rates in other ICs. Attrition data and projections within ICs and in positions across ICs also inform the strategic recruitment strategy. High attrition in a position where the qualifications are common across multiple ICs can be mitigated by issuing global announcements instead of announcements for specific ICs. That way, the time and resources invested in seeking out candidates for the position can potentially benefit several ICs.

Just as the CSD's improvements in operational HR support were made with consistent effort through multiple phases, the reputation of the HR team as a strategic advisor and partner developed over time. OHR has kept its focus on continual improvement, which has been essential in maintaining a high level of service in a constantly evolving environment. Although a variety of factors contributed to the results of this ongoing effort, Phil notes that if he had to identify a single thing that made all of it possible, it would be support and resources from the top. Chris and Phil had the trust of the NIH leadership, who were confident in allocating the appropriate resources for the transformation to be successful. NIH leaders had confidence in the return that OHR would deliver in terms of improved services for the investment of resources.

Results

Since the NIH human capital transformation was a steady, gradual effort, the results of these initiatives emerged over time. Results clearly show that the continued effort and investment have paid off for NIH.

Improved Customer Service

During the Austin project, customers and stakeholders from the ICs gave OHR a wealth of information on what they needed from CSD, and OHR followed through on meeting those needs. For example, when it became clear that many ICs wanted their on-site HR specialists back, OHR worked with the ICs to make this happen in a way that satisfied both individual IC needs and higher level HR priorities. This effort represented a basic foundational level of providing tailored customer service: The customers made a request, and OHR did its best to accommodate them.

At a more strategic level, HR leadership used the high-level feedback gathered through the Austin project to propose and implement specific initiatives to address gaps in customer satisfaction. When the ICs asked for better accountability, OHR built accountability mechanisms in throughout the organization structure and the performance management program.

Phil and Chris had often been approached by IC executive officers with complaints about the lack of HR services to meet their needs. As a result of these projects, Chris describes a clear change in customer perceptions of HR: "After these projects and the emphasis on strategic leadership in OHR, the complaints died down and we would get compliments on the work the OHR staff did—quicker hiring, better candidates, faster service, creative ideas, more responsive staff."

Improved Operational Outcomes

Between 2009 and 2012, NIH reduced its time to hire from 106 to 62 days—a 40 percent decrease. The average time to issue a certificate of eligible candidates to managers after an announcement closed decreased from 21 days in 2008 to 8 days in 2012—more than a 60 percent decrease. In addition, the average time to make a job offer to the manager's selected candidate decreased from 3 days in 2008 to the same day in 2012. The strategic recruitment meetings, CSD organization, and overall focus on customer service have clearly played a role in this operational outcome.

Other creative initiatives have contributed to the HR department's success in improving outcomes as well. For example, HR implemented global recruiting and shared certificates for common positions. These programs streamlined the hiring process by filling common vacancies across NIH using one announcement and by allowing hiring managers to share applicants with other hiring managers who needed to fill a similar position. The number of hires through global recruitment increased from 164 in 2010 to 470 in 2012.

Successful Functioning as Strategic Partners

OHR has successfully established a strategic partnership with NIH leadership to provide analytic and advisory services for NIH's human capital programs and processes. As HR demonstrated its value on more and more projects and initiatives, the NIH director and executive team began to seek out its services more frequently and to rely more heavily on OHR guidance and support. OHR is also a driver of strategic direction. Its proactive consultation, combined with the agile responsiveness of the SIG, provides comprehensive coverage of NIH's human capital needs.

"Restoring the quality of human resource functions was a priority for NIH after the major staff reduction and the loss of seasoned leaders that resulted from the initial consolidation," says Colleen Barros, NIH deputy director for management. "At NIH, the Office of Human Resources is considered a mission-critical function. We invested in the organization and derived results that make us the leader in delivering customer service and strategic thinking. When I talk to my colleagues in other federal agencies, I hear complaints about their HR services; complaints that we eliminated or reduced years ago. I am proud of our team and what they have accomplished. I rely on them for strategic advice for enterprisewide issues and count on them to deliver the best possible creative services to the institutes and centers."

What It All Means 14

Ellen Tunstall
John Salamone

There you have it—our 13 stories, insights actually, into what works in government. We promised up front that we wouldn't be prescriptive, that we would try to avoid trendiness, that we'd share some of the messiness, and, most important, that we'd tell you what happened and why. We hope we've accomplished that.

President Theodore Roosevelt is often credited with building the foundation of the modern civil service. His words, and the words of others, highlight five themes and lessons we have gleaned from our study and conversations.

Foundations of Modern Government

"During Roosevelt's 7 years as President, the foundations of the modern Federal Government were laid. Many new agencies were created to perform functions for which the need had long existed. It was a period of major governmental expansion. A Reclamation Act, establishing irrigation projects, was passed in 1902. A Department of Commerce and Labor was created in 1903. A Pure Food and Drugs Act and a Federal Meat Inspection Act were passed in 1906, and Roosevelt added almost 150,000,000 acres of public lands to the 45,000,000 acres set aside as public conservation areas by his three predecessors. This expansion increased the necessity of obtaining more efficient organization and administration of functions of the executive branch...."

Biography of an Ideal, U.S. Office of Personnel Management (http://archive.opm.gov/BiographyofAnIdeal/PDF/BiographyOfAnIdeal.pdf)

1. *Analyze and plan.* The longest serving First Lady of the United States—Anna Eleanor Roosevelt—said, "It takes as much energy to wish as it does to plan."[1] In our research, every successful organization recognized its problems and challenges. The organizations didn't simply wish things would get better or look the other way. They collected and analyzed data and used those data to identify issues. NSF measured turnover and determined that "rotators" from universities and colleges contributed to a higher-than-expected rate. USAID identified workload drivers and found a way to link them to workforce requirements.

   Once the agencies identified issues, they looked for solutions and planned for success. Some organizations, like SSA, used a sophisticated and formal approach to identify and plan "strategic and tactical" initiatives to improve knowledge management. At NARA, the director knew her HR department excelled at high-touch, personalized customer service, perhaps to the detriment of efficiency. Once she discovered why, she made a plan and set goals that transformed personnel servicing and guided the transition to an improved HR system. Consider also the ways NASA regularly looked at its business processes and policies to drive long-range and large-scale changes and better meet its needs.

2. *Be decisive—take action.* Teddy Roosevelt said, "In any moment of decision, the best thing you can do is the right thing, the next best thing is the wrong thing, and the worst thing you can do is nothing."[2] The agencies we studied took action, moved forward, and made a difference. Consider the efforts of Phil Lenowitz at NIH. As the Deputy Director of HR, he and his team identified actionable steps and implemented a large-scale undertaking that resulted in substantial improvements to service delivery. Similarly, VA for VETS demonstrates the effectiveness of an integrated approach that combines multiple components and actions to achieve success. The program achieved its goal of hiring more veterans by leveraging virtual job fairs, career coaching, training,

hiring process reforms, onboarding, and mentoring programs to impact veteran hiring and retention positively.

Sometimes being decisive and taking action can be arduous and time-consuming. USPTO is one of the most successful federal agencies to address and resolve challenges by leveraging technology and adopting a new way to work. It took 15 years and multiple iterations of a pilot, but by using telework, USPTO found a winning combination that attracts the talent it needs, keeps its physical footprint in bounds, and accomplishes its mission.

3. *Find a champion.* Another theme, perhaps the most critical, is leadership. In every successful endeavor, we found a leader or group of leaders who took responsibility and championed change. Think about Cal Scovel, Transportation's Inspector General. His "mission people" philosophy was critical in improving leadership across the organization. Similarly, Robert Hosenfeld's creativity and leadership guided his CBP team in realizing dramatic staffing improvements. NGA's bold shift to a new personnel system with pay bands and performance pay would not have been possible without the strong and consistent leadership of its directors; their commitment left no doubt about NGA's vision for the future and the direction the agency would take.

    Once again, President Roosevelt supplied the perfect descriptor: "People ask the difference between a leader and a boss. The leader works in the open, and the boss is covert. The leader leads, and the boss drives."[3] Roosevelt also said, "The best executive is one who has sense enough to pick good people to do what he wants done, and self-restraint enough to keep from meddling with them while they do it."[4]

    Government that works needs effective leaders!

4. *Measure success.* President Roosevelt said, "The most important single ingredient in the formula of success is knowing how to get along with people."[5] He also said,

"All the resources we need are in the mind."[6] Both of those statements still ring true, but in today's competitive marketplace, we also need to define success, measure it, and replicate it. What more practical example could there be than the Air Force Research Laboratory, which for 15 years has driven mission success by measuring employee performance and compensating employees more when they contribute more? Consider how NIH measured and replicated improvements in customer service, operational outcomes, and strategic partnerships. And what about CVM? Without measurement and evaluation, the center would likely not have had a way to continually enhance employee engagement practices.

It's interesting that many of the stories tell a tale of flexibility. The successful agencies, when they consider their success, weren't dogmatic about the solution. They measured the impact so they could learn what wasn't working and then redirect, change, and improve it. Sometimes the solution went well beyond the original idea. VA is a great example. Its focus on career development was supported by empirically based research that illustrated the power of engaging and developing the workforce. VA considered its options, found a champion, and took action. More than that, VA measured success at every step on the path to MyCareer@VA. The agency analyzed needs, validated content, evaluated usability, talked to users, gauged impact, and measured use and satisfaction. VA made modifications along the way toward an innovative, successful program that impacts organizational effectiveness.

5. *Believe.* Individuals can and do make a difference. They provide service and deliver results for the people of our nation. Even in the toughest economic and political times, federal employees deliver time and time again. They believe in public service and deliver great results.

We'll give President Roosevelt the final word: "Believe you can and you're halfway there."[7]

NOTES

1   http://thinkexist.com/quotation/it_takes_as_much_energy_to_wish_as_it_
does_to/186924.html.

2   http://kenfran.tripod.com/teddy.htm.

3   Ibid.

4   Ibid.

5   Ibid.

6   Ibid.

7   http://theodorerooseveltclub.com/index.php/theodore-roosevelts-legacy.

About the Authors

Nathan Bailey, PhD
Chapters 11 and 12

Nathan Bailey is a vice president at FMP, focusing on technology and HR transformation projects. He has worked extensively with federal agencies to evaluate, develop, and enhance the systems they use to support HR service delivery.

Tim Barnhart
Chapters 1, 5, 6, and 10

Tim Barnhart is the president and founder of FMP. He has worked with a number of agencies on contribution-based compensation systems, flexible work initiatives, and strategies for program implementation and change.

Jenna Bender
Chapter 3

Jenna Bender is a consultant at FMP, focusing on career development, strategic communications, and training.

Jessica Dzieweczynski, PhD
Chapters 1 and 4

Jessica Dzieweczynski is a senior consultant at FMP, specializing in leadership development and employee onboarding. She has worked closely with federal clients to design, develop, implement, and evaluate employee onboarding programs.

Alexis Gray
Chapters 11 and 12

Alexis Gray is a consultant at FMP. Her areas of expertise include organizational assessment, strategic planning, and HR transformation.

Carolyn Kurowski
Chapters 2, 8, and 9

Carolyn Kurowski is a senior vice president at FMP. She has worked with a number of agencies to design and implement innovative workforce tools and programs.

Dawn Flaherty Lavelle
Chapter 8

Dawn Flaherty Lavelle of Lavelle Associates provides consulting and project management expertise in the areas of organizational change and effectiveness. She has worked extensively with private and public sector entities.

Danny McGeehan
Chapter 4

Daniel McGeehan is a consultant at FMP. He has worked closely with the Center for Veterinary Medicine, partnering with the human capital management staff on a number of initiatives, including employee onboarding, competency modeling, and the creation of a strategic human capital plan.

Mike McManus
Chapters 3, 5, 9, and 10

Mike McManus is a senior advisor at FMP and a recognized expert in compensation and performance management strategies and practices.

Sherean Miller
Chapter 6

Sherean Miller is a senior vice president at FMP. She has worked with dozens of federal agencies to implement a broad range of management consulting initiatives.

Jessica Milloy
Chapter 4

Jessica Milloy is a managing consultant at FMP, focusing on organizational development, learning and development, and strategic workforce planning. She has worked closely with a number of organizations to enhance their onboarding processes, leadership development programs, and organizational effectiveness.

Maggie Moore
Chapter 4

Maggie Moore is a senior consultant at FMP. She has worked extensively with agencies to design, develop, and implement innovative onboarding programs to enhance new employee productivity and engagement.

Kathryn Newcomer, PhD
Foreword

Kathryn Newcomer is the Director of the Trachtenberg School of Public Policy and Public Administration at the George Washington University. She teaches public and nonprofit, program evaluation, research design, and applied statistics, and has published five books. Dr. Newcomer is a fellow of the National Academy of Public Administration and is on the board of the American Evaluation Association.

Erin Pitera
Preface

Erin Pitera is the senior vice president and chief operating officer of FMP. She provides leadership in the execution of strategies for client relationships, business growth, human capital, and infrastructure. Her knowledge and expertise include strategic human capital planning, workforce planning, talent management, learning and development, organizational transformation, and evaluation.

Ben Porr, PhD
Chapter 8

Ben Porr is a managing consultant at FMP. He is a practicing industrial and organizational psychologist who focuses on the strategic and tactical implementation of human capital initiatives.

Ashley Agerter Raitor
Chapter 2

Ashley Agerter Raitor is a senior consultant at FMP. She has worked closely with USAID for over five years, partnering with the HR organization to develop, enhance, and institutionalize the agency's consolidated workforce planning model and related processes.

John Salamone
Chapters 7 and 14

John Salamone is a vice president at FMP. He has served in a variety of capacities in the executive and legislative branches of government.

Lisa Sper
Chapter 1

Lisa Sper is a vice president at FMP. She has over 20 years of experience as an HR practitioner and consultant in both the private and public sectors.

Glenn Sutton
Chapters 3, 11, 12, and 13

Glenn Sutton is a senior advisor at FMP. He has had an extensive career in federal human resources, information technology, and management consulting.

Paul Thompson
Chapter 7

Paul Thompson is a human resources consultant and a recognized expert on performance management and senior executive service policies and programs. He retired from federal service after a distinguished career at the Office of Personnel Management.

Ellen Tunstall
Chapter 14

Ellen Tunstall is a senior advisor at FMP and has a long career as an HR professional and leader. As a senior executive, she led OPM and DoD organizations. She is adjunct staff with the RAND corporation and a National Academy of Public Administration fellow.

Cristina Wilcox
Chapter 13

Cristina Wilcox is a consultant at FMP. She has worked with several federal agencies on organizational assessment and strategic human capital initiatives.

Index

KPI. *See* key performance
    indicator

L

labor-management relations/
    employee relations (LR/ER),
    110. *See also* knowledge
    management
leaders, developing
    360 degree assessments, 4
    coaching, 4–5
    communication, 9–10
    culture change, 5–6
    DOT Office of Inspector
      General, 1–2
    employee viewpoint survey,
      2–3
    internal leadership and support,
      12–14
    keys to success, 5
    leadership planning and col-
      laboration, 8–9
    mentoring, 8
    organizational assessments,
      10–12
    organizational climate, 14–15
    performance culture, 9
    reasons for success, 15–16
    return on investment, 14
    training, 6–8
    vision, 1–2
    workforce retention, 14
LR/ER. *See* labor-management
    relations/employee relations

N

NAAS. *See* NASA automated
    awards system
NARA. *See* National Archives and
    Records Administration
NASA. *See* National Aeronautics
    and Space Administration
NASA automated awards system
    (NAAS), 185
NASA Employee Benefits System
    (NEBS), 180, 185

NASA organizational profile sys-
    tem (NOPS), 186
NASA Personnel Payroll System
    (NPPS), 180
National Aeronautics and Space
    Administration (NASA),
    177–178. *See also* human
    resource technology
National Archives and Records
    Administration (NARA),
    163–165. *See also* human
    resource service delivery
National Geospatial-Intelligence
    Agency (NGA), 121–122.
    See also human resource
    systems
National Institutes of Health
    (NIH), 195–198. *See also* hu-
    man resources customer and
    strategic services
National Intelligence Civilian
    Compensation Program
    (NICCP), 135
National Park Service (NPS), 59
National Science Foundation
    (NSF), 52–53. *See also* new
    employees, integrating
NEBS. *See* NASA Employee
    Benefits System
New Employee Orientation
    (NEO), 54
new employees, integrating
    clarification, 51, 56–57
    compliance, 51, 53–55
    connection, 51, 58
    culture, 51, 57–58
    evaluations, 60
    executives, support for, 58–60
    findings, 63
    National Science Foundation,
      52–53
    orientation *versus* onboarding,
      49–51
    success, measuring, 61–63
new executive transition (NExT),
    55